A NEWBURY CHILDHOOD

Mamma and Daddy

A
Newbury Childhood

JOAN BOOKER

BERKSHIRE COUNTY LIBRARY

FIRST PUBLISHED 1982

Printed and designed by
Berkshire County Council Reprographics Unit

ISBN 0 9506044 3 7

TO MY PARENTS

FOREWORD

This book began as a writing exercise undertaken with the Newbury Writers' Group which meets in Newbury Library on Saturday afternoons. Our tutor was Maureen Duffy, Writer-in-Residence. The work undertaken soon ceased to be a chore and became an absorbing interest.

In group work there must always be a sense of gratitude to the members of the group for indulgence in listening and for encouragement, and I would like to thank my Saturday afternoon friends for these. I am grateful to my family for exercising their memories in search of the answers to my questions about our past, and to Mrs. Pat Harding for helping me with the typing.

I would also like to thank Berkshire County Library for making publication possible, and Southern Arts for sending us our Writer-in-Residence in May 1981. My special thanks are due to Maureen Duffy herself, without whose advice, support and active help this book would never have been produced.

Joan Booker

THE ILLUSTRATIONS

Frontispiece

Between pages 8 - 9

Between pages 48 - 49

Between pages 88 - 89

The cover picture 'Lucy in the Cornfield' and numbers 1 - 4, 6 - 8, and 10 were taken by the author's father, Henry A. Torpey.

CHAPTER ONE

For the first eighteen months of my life I lived with my parents and my older sister, Lucy, in Grandma's old house in Craven Street. The First World War was just over, and my father, a stranger to me, had recently been demobbed. We had as yet no home of our own. The old house in Craven Street is now a junk shop, and demolition has already set in at the end of the row.

Each back garden of this short terrace had a tall, narrow wooden gate with a latch, giving onto an untidy little access lane. The house, by hind-sight, was inconvenient, dark and cold, requiring cleaning out of all proportion to the comfort it gave, but it was fascinating to the two small girls. The front door opened onto a long, poorly-lit passage, linoleum-covered and wonderful for sliding in our socks when we were older. There was a second staircase to the attic, full of apples and junk. It had both kitchen and scullery, and a huge, walk-in larder which would be the envy of many housewives in small houses today. The house seemed full of aunties and uncles, as indeed it was. My mother was the eldest of her family, and few of the teenaged siblings had yet left home.

My mother gave us a banana to share one day.

"Let your sister do it. She's bigger than you."

We scrambled up to the wide bit of landing where the stairs turned, to divide our treasure. Lucy peeled it, broke it, and gave me a very small portion.

"Because you're smaller." she told me.

This is my first recollection of the injustice of life.

Soon after this we moved into a council house on a new estate. The houses, built to the post-war ideal of 'homes fit for heroes', were grouped around a large central green. We had a garden front and back, a good stone-built shed, bathroom properly equipped, an integral coal-shed with a rainwater tap, with its entrance under the same brick-built porch which sheltered the back door.

At first I was not happy. I can recall my distress at the expanses of grey walls, the wide areas of cold new linoleum, the bedroom with nothing in it but Lucy's iron bedstead and my green metal cot, the smell of paint and distemper. I longed for the hugger-mugger of eight people and their possessions which had formed a protective layer around me in my first home. Our garden was a humpy, much-trodden bit of field bounded on three sides by a strand-wire fence.

There were strange, big children living near us who made us shy, and who endlessly lifted me up and passed me round. The house next door was not yet finished, and the big children would sit on the half-built walls, and sometimes even walk on them. It frequently happened that I was lifted up to sit with them on the wall, where I sat very, very still, aware of the three-foot drop below me. One afternoon I was horrified to see them all jump off the wall as one man to follow another friend who had just appeared. Stranded high and lonely on that rough, red brickwork I was utterly panic-stricken, and my screams brought my mother running to the rescue. When my sobbing had subsided she put me in the pram for a rest, in the yard just outside the back door. Having no wish to sleep I grizzled and complained, so she patiently lifted me out and set me down to play. She was busy, however, and could not spare time to amuse me, so when I thought how safe and comfortable I had been in the pram I asked to be lifted back in.

"Oh, no," she said, "I'm not keeping on. You had your chance."

Small as I was, I was quite able to see the reasonableness of her reply.

The fine summer days of that first year in our new house helped me to settle and accept the move. I grew to love the humpy, broken-bricky back garden for its quietness and for its treasures. Lucy and I found little bits of sawn wood, nails, screws, bits of sandpaper, even the head of an old paint-brush. But better than any of these were my private treasures, the scarlet pimpernels, chickweed, mayweed, daisies, buttercups, dandelions, the dozens of low-growing flowering weeds which seed on any open waste ground. These were my own flowers; no-one else wanted them. My sister Lucy walked on them, but I was small enough to be very close to them physically, and loved them dearly, as I still do.

The strand-wire fence separated our piece of the rough field from the unspoilt grassland beyond. We very soon learned to stand on the lower wire and hold the one above us and bounce, which was fun, until our parents pointed out that we were stretching the wire and spoiling the fence, and forbade us to do it. But the wires were already bent, and the space between them already wider, so we two little girls sometimes crept through the gap. On the other side of the fence was a different world, a real grassy field with green hedges and flowers tall enough to pick, flowers which even Lucy appreciated. It was a strange sensation to see our familiar house from this novel viewpoint, almost a feeling of disloyalty at having come away.

Our little ventures were soon discovered.

"I don't think you girls should go through the fence, you know," my mother told us. "It's not our field."

"They won't hurt," my father told her, "As long as they stay where we can see them. It's all going to be built over soon. They might as well enjoy it while it's still there."

The field in which we were playing eventually became that row of neat houses and gardens which form the newer side of Craven Road, where later on I had friends living.

My father was a highly skilled carpenter and joiner, employed on the half-built council estate where we lived. The temporary works office, with an outside counter, was set up in a corner of the green, and on Saturday, which was half-day and pay-day he would take Lucy by the hand and me in his arms and walk across the green to collect his wages. I can clearly remember the handful of silver and copper and the two gold sovereigns which seemed adequate to support the family for a week.

My father was most conscious of the need to care for his tools, which were the source of his income, a trait due partly to training and partly to temperament. The commodious shed was soon fitted up with a carpenter's bench and vice, and racks for the tools. The sounds of hammer and saw, sandpaper and plane were the closest of the sounds which drifted through our open window into the bedroom on summer evenings. We thrived on the smells of wood and boiling glue, and hung wooden shavings round our straight little fringes of hair for golden ringlets. We were happy and secure.

This state of settled and complete happiness did not last for long. My mother decided that the family exchequer could do with some help, and she took a post as cashier in a large local sweet-shop. A big girl, called Gladys, was appointed to look after us at home. Gladys was, perhaps, fourteen, and completely inexperienced, and in fact the change meant that we were hauled about with the older girls at their play more than ever. Wherever they wanted to go we were taken. Occasionally Gladys had shopping to do, so we were changed into our best dresses and wheeled into the town in the pram.

These best dresses had been knitted by one of our many kind aunts of a very bright pink, very shiny heavy silk. The colour and texture delighted me, but they were cold and slithery to a warm little body. Now I had no objection to my mother sliding me into the pink silk, but protested with a storm of tears at Gladys doing it. On this occasion whilst in town Gladys went into the sweet-shop to speak to our mother, who was delighted to see us and found a few sweets for us all.

"She's been a very naughty girl," Gladys announced, nodding towards my end of the pram. "She wouldn't let me dress her."

I adored my mother, dreaded her disapproval, and longed to explain that for her I would not have been naughty. Gladys shared the sweets on the way home, giving the odd one to Lucy "because she was a good girl". But far more than sweets I wanted my mother to come home with us, and to send Gladys away. To me the situation was incomprehensible.

Those bright pink dresses had a future. When they became too small they were unpicked, skeined and washed for re-use. But the slippery yarn was never used. It lay about in the cupboard for years, looked at and handled by us, until it became tangled into a muddly bundle. Whenever Lucy and I needed to tie something up, or to make a school satchel from a paper bag and string, this was the 'string' we used. It made us belts, bows for our slippers, hair ribbons for our dolls, and was our standby as a source of unlimited tying material for years. A more intractible yarn for small children's use could hardly be imagined, but this we did not realise.

This first separation from our mother did not last long. Littler Peter was born on Christmas Day when I was two-and-a-half years old. We had not been told that a baby was on the way, and were totally taken by surprise, but both Lucy and I were excited by the new arrival. Since our mother was in bed during this Christmas, people were more than usually kind to us for reasons I did not understand. I spent a lot of time in our parents' room, strangely anxious to keep contact with them both, and with the new baby. When he was about three days old Lucy and I went into the bedroom after dinner and saw some things on the bed, glittering in the pale sunshine of a winter's afternoon. There were some chocolate animals in silver paper and two rolled-up picture books.

"Here's something for you," Mamma said. "Mrs Jennings sent them from her Christmas tree. Wasn't that kind?"

"Yes very kind," I thought, as I peeled a chocolate lion.

"What's a Christmas tree?" I asked.

"A tree with presents on." answered my four-and-a-half year old sister briefly.

Even at that age I could not really believe in a tree which grew presents, so I withdrew into the easily accessible world of magic, where the mysterious Christmas tree could both grow, as trees did, and offer children sweets without the need to conform to my few known facts. Christmas meant little to me that year. I had no notion of its universality, and with Mamma in bed we had little of its fun.

By the following year our garden contained several rows of unprosperous cabbages and a row of peas, which fed the wild birds but not us. My father was never interested in gardening, and our patch became pleasantly matured without planning. Eventually the remaining humps were roughly levelled and sown with grass seed, which meant that for the rest of that year we had to play either in our gravel yard, or in the 'field' beyond. Thus my garden of tiny flowers was gone. I gazed upon the uninterestingly uniform spears of new grass with a sense of loss. Already, at three, I had a past, and knew the taste of nostalgia. But the growing blades themselves brought me a new and lasting wonder in their tender, brilliant green, and their gentle kiss upon soft flesh as I stooped down and swept my arms over them.

It must have been about now that my father made our first swing in the garden. Once he had bought the right lengths of wood it was for him a quick and simple job to erect the frame, neat and strong and smooth. He was a perfectionist, and everything he made was well-finished as well as perfect in function. We watched him screw the two semi-spiral holders into the cross-bar and hitch the rope over them. Then he produced the smooth wooden seat whose slots exactly fitted the double dangling loops. He had the first swing himself, then it was my mother's turn. Lucy got on next, and then at last it was my go. Carefully they sat me up on the seat, and very gently moved me to and fro, calling out,

"Hold the rope! Hold tight. Hold on!"

The injunction was quite unnecessary. There is no grip tighter than that of a small, rather nervous child.

CHAPTER TWO

Winter came round again, and one night in December Lucy and I were awoken in the middle of the night by strange noises. The house had been quiet for hours so we knew it was not our parents going to bed.

"Burglars," said Lucy, and we cowered in our sheets, afraid even to call out. Then we heard Daddy's voice talking, and Mamma answering, so our first dreadful fear subsided. The next unusual sound was a ring at the front doorbell, and strange footsteps mounting the stairs. A third voice joined the quiet conversation, so we decided that we could safely get out of bed and investigate. But we were turned away from the bedroom door by Daddy, who hustled us back to our beds.

"Who's that other lady, Daddy? Why did she come in the middle of the night?"

"It's only Nurse Hawdon. You know her. She's come because Mamma can't get to sleep. You're not to get out any more now or I'll be cross. I'm going to pin up a big blanket over your door to make it quiet for you. Now go to sleep."

He kissed us both, and we lay obediently quiet, listening as he fixed the blanket across our door with drawing pins.

In the morning it was Daddy who came to wake us and to help us dress.

"What do you think?" he asked. "You've got a new baby sister!"

Now we understood the reason for the disturbed night. The nurse had, quite unexpectedly, brought a baby. How kind of her! As soon as we were ready we were allowed to go in and see Mamma, sitting up in bed with the baby in her arms.

"What's her name?"

"Norma. Do you like that name?"

"Yes." I thought on the whole Nurse Hawdon had chosen well.

Both of our parents had been one of eight children, so they did not consider that four little ones constituted a large family. Nevertheless, we were a taxing delight to them. Money was never very plentiful, and Mamma was not always well. This made me, and I suppose the others, sad and anxious about her. Deaths from tuberculosis were then a commonplace among young people. My father had lost a brother and a sister from this illness, both at the age of nineteen, so he and my mother had to grapple with fears and anxieties of which we children were thought to know nothing. But I lay awake many a night, oppressed by a terrible clair-voyance, and especially so after one of our happy family picnics.

These picnics, undertaken with no transport save the pram, were the high spots of our lives. On fine Sunday mornings in Summer we would set off about half past ten along the Enborne Road to a field which we called 'our field'. Sandwiches and apples filled the well of the pram, now doing service for the fourth baby, and often for a leg-weary toddler as well. The lemonade bottle rolled about on the bottom of this big, old-fashioned pram with a fine rumbling sound, and we were constantly anxious lest the cup should get broken. We took only one cup, and of course there were no tissues or rolls of kitchen paper. My father wiped the lip of the cup after each drinker with a fresh leaf, sacramentally. For some reason there was never more than one bottle of lemonade between the four hot, bounding children, and we were always crazed with thirst when it was time to go home. The energy and delight we had displayed on the morning walk changed by evening to weariness and whining. The road seemed twice as long at the end of the day.

It was these homeward walks of the future which I foresaw with such painful clarity. I imagined us coming home, tired out, with only Daddy in charge pushing the pram, carrying his heavy camera, and having no-one to talk to except grumbling children.

It was about now, too, that another worry raised its head. We all had whooping-cough, quite badly, and Peter perhaps, worse than all of us. It had changed him from a chubby, angelic baby to a slim, fretful little boy with no appetite. His dislike of food was something I could never understand. The rest of us had sufficient for health, but there was no surplus, and no high feeding. Peter had his potatoes mashed with milk, but he did not like that. They mashed them with butter, but he still would not eat. He cried all through mealtimes, which was miserable to hear, and he ungratefully refused titbits which the rest of us would have liked. Daddy came in from work one evening and sat him on his knee.

"Look, Peter. I've brought you some chocolate."

It was a twopenny bar, purple-wrapped and unbroken, an unheard-of luxury for just one child. Mamma opened it and offered it to Peter, who turned his head aside with a fretful gesture.

Lucy and I had for some time agreed that Peter was his father's favourite, and spoiled. We were both a little jealous of the attention he was given, and the little extras with which his appetite was tempted.

"I wish I could have that." I said, very much fearing that the chocolate would be messed about and thrown away with other rejected delicacies. "Why does Peter have to have so many treats? He's always having nice things."

"Peter is not well, Jane, you know that. You can eat everything, so it's very unkind of you to talk like that. Don't say any more about it."

Lucy, with whom these thoughts had more than half originated, had said nothing. She was still a 'kind' little girl.

Peter recovered from this illness and was buoyant for a short time, and then fell poorly again. He was a delicate child, and a clever one, the apple of his father's eye. At the age of three he was fascinated by seeing Daddy shave, and would shriek with joy when he dabbed him on the nose with the soapy shaving brush. Daddy gave him an old brush, some soap and a mug of warm water, and with a towel tied in and tucked around his neck the little boy would lather his face all over. This was such a happy game for them both that Daddy took it a stage further and made him a wooden cut-throat razor, a replica of his own, so smooth and perfectly shaped that I was lost in admiration of his skill. Then Peter could really scrape his face and wipe his razor off on the rag, whilst the family stood around him, delighted with his earnest mimicry.

In his absorbtion with his son Daddy did not forget his little daughters. Lucy and I played school endlessly, sitting on our small wooden stools, and using the seats of the Windsor chairs as desks. To our great delight we were presented with a secretly made real blackboard and easel, exactly like the school one but child-sized. It added a new dimension to our play, and gave the teacher a new dignity.

This was a highly productive period for the skilful hands in the garden shed. There issued from it, in quick succession, a drop-side cot, a high chair, a kitchen cupboard, a duckboard, a fine chest of drawers with all corners rounded, and boxes and shelves wherever needed. His craftmanship set standards for his children which have given us all a critical eye for quality of work, and a dislike of shoddy products.

CHAPTER THREE

I have no recollection of the day when Lucy started school, but I have interesting odd memories of the time when I was left at home to play alone. Peter was too small to be a companion, dearly as I loved him, so although I had the swing all to myself, and 'Joyce', and the rag book, I missed Lucy very much. Joyce was a soft toy of the most ordinary kind, a grey, sitting-up rabbit, which belonged to us both. It was our first choice for the baby when playing mothers and fathers. The rag book was another shared possession. Its cotton pages bore pictures and stories of the animals leaving their ark to go on a Sunday School outing, but to us it was of more value as a pillow, a blanket, a shawl, nappie or towel, according to Joyce's requirements of the moment. But when, on school days, I had Joyce without fear of her being snatched or argued away from me, the joy of possession waned.

There were enrichments, however, which Lucy's new experience brought to our playing at weekends and in holidays. I never tired of hearing what went on within those mysterious walls called school, things said, and things done by teachers, by children, how good they all had to be, how they feared terrible punishments. She brought home new knowledge and skills, stories, songs and poems which I begged her to repeat over and over again. When, at Christmas, she was chosen to be a fairy, with wings, crown and wand, my envy knew no bounds. I could not wait to get to school myself.

I really could not wait. I ran away one day and followed Lucy to school when she was returning for the afternoon session. It was a summer day, and I was playing with my sister outside our house until it was time for her to leave. Several of her friends came along and Lucy joined them for the ten-minute walk to school, out of the avenue, over the railway bridge, along Pound Street and over the road to the Council School. I just tagged along behind them, unnoticed for a while, but once over the bridge I was spotted.

"There's your little sister, Lucy. Tell her to go home."

"She'll get lost." another friend suggested, hopefully.

'Getting lost' was a classic, story-book situation, guaranteed to provide some excitement.

"Go home, Jane. Mamma will be cross."

They travelled on, but were well aware of me a short distance behind them, and secretly a little thrilled by my dreadful badness. They tried running ahead, but I ran too, and although they could not shake me off they started to widen the gap.

Lucy began to fear I might really get lost.

"I'd better take her home." she said nervously.

"You'll get into trouble. We'll be ever so late."

So we all went on, and were soon at school. I hung around Lucy as she joined her class line in the playground, and was immediately spotted by her teacher, Miss Hartly.

"Is this your little sister, Lucy?"

"Yes, teacher. She followed us. We told her to go home but she wouldn't."

"Well, you'd better see what Miss King says. Go and take her now, before lessons."

Lucy took my hand and led me off to the dreaded presence. I had heard so much from Lucy and her friends about this tartar of a headmistress, about her keeping children in after school, about her cane hidden in the cupboard, and how

7

'strick' she was, that by now I was very nervous. We entered the hall, and there, seated at her desk, was the sweetest grey-haired old lady I had ever seen. She must have been under sixty, but to me she looked about eighty. She had gentle, blue eyes and a kind, low voice. I trusted her at once.

"Well, Jane," she said quietly, "Don't you think you were rather naughty to run away like that? Your poor mother will be so worried."

I had not thought of that.

"If I let you stay with Lucy this afternoon will you promise me not to follow her again?"

I nodded.

"She always wants to go to school with me." Lucy volunteered. I remember thinking that she seemed to be on very friendly terms with this tyrant.

"Well, you go along with Lucy now, and don't interrupt her work, will you? Then we'll see."

I had no disruptive intentions whatsoever. My respect for the mystery of lessons was tremendous. The afternoon passed quickly and happily, and all I saw delighted me. At last I was seeing the inside of school. As we filed out of the classroom Miss King took Lucy and me aside for a moment.

"Miss Hartly tells me you have been a very good little girl, Jane. Do you want to come to school every day?"

I nodded with enthusiasm.

"Well, I've written a note to your mother which Lucy will carry, and if she agrees you can start tomorrow. But you must understand that you cannot be in Lucy's class. You will have to go in the baby room with Miss Farmer."

I nodded again. I knew exactly what she meant. Being separated from Lucy would be no problem at all for me.

When we arrived home with the note our mother had only just missed me. She was machining nighties for us from stiff, unbleached calico which had scratchy brown specks in it. Our nighties were always made from this material and were never comfortable until they got old. Mamma had been so engrossed that she had not noticed the passing of time. She read the note, gladly accepted what it offered, and then remembered to reprove me for naughtiness.

The next day, at four years and one month old I started on my long school career.

I had expected to like it, and I did. The big children in Lucy's class had dual desks, with two inexplicable round holes in the top. The baby class sat at tables for two, in small wooden armchairs with arm-rests, like semi-circular fences. The Infant School, now modified and used as St. Nicholas' Annexe, was alongside the railway, and the shriek of trains has ever since reminded me of early reading books. Since the cookery department was over the Infant School and reached by the fire escape, each class of plain cooks on its way up to or down from instruction signalled its passing with a clatter of Blakey's boot protectors on the iron staircase.

On that first morning I made my way up the wide, shallow steps with all the gravity of a cathedral visitor. At the inner door I was met by an unrecognisable, strong smell, emanating, it soon became clear, from the squashy dabs of very red carbolic soap on the ledge of the sink. Although my clean-from-home hands did not need washing I was swept along with a bunch of children all eager, it seemed, for a hygienic start to the day. I soon saw why. The first to reach it turned a handle on the wall and the water gushed out in two long rows of tiny jets, curving over like

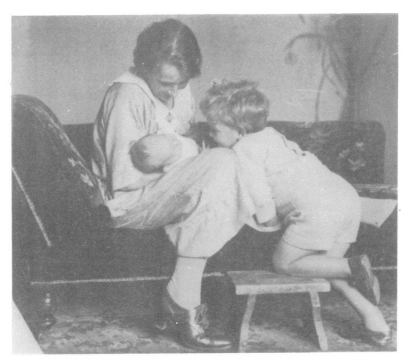

Mamma and Peter with baby Norma

Harvesting at Enborne

Jane reading to Lucy and Peter from the rag book

Newbury Market Place

sea waves and splashing into the sink, a wonderful plaything for children. I put my hands under the jets and laughed; each tiny stream was warm and gentle, and collectively they tickled. But there was no time for play. We had to go in.

Our names were called out in alphabetical order, except mine, which had been added at the bottom. Each child answered, "Yes, Miss Farmer". Very few were absent. We filed quietly into the hall and sang a hymn with Miss Farmer playing the piano. I did not know the hymn so I gazed about me at all the children, the stuffed birds in the glass case, the zig-zag block flooring, the pictures on the wall, one of the king and queen and one of Captain Oates walking out into the snow. We put our hands together and shut our eyes to say 'Our Father' and 'I believe', after which each silent class filed back to a closed classroom to be seen no more until playtime. Lucy gave me a friendly wave before she disappeared, but I pretended not to see. I was an independent school-child, and needed no sistering.

Back in the baby room we were all soon happily engaged in what the timetable used to call 'occupations'. A few children played quietly with the sand-tray, another group had button fastening, others were doing paper weaving with coloured mats. There were shape-sorting sets, bead threaders and easy puzzles, all based on the Montessori sense-training methods. This must have been something fairly new in English education.

My particular occupation on this first day was boot-lacing and tying. I had a board on which was a leather boot-opening with eyelets, and two long laces fastened to the top holes. This was quite a problem for a young four-year old, and Miss Farmer soon noticed my lack of progress down the opening.

"Never mind, Jane. If you can't tie it up just thread the laces through the holes."

I was greatly relieved, and did what I could. My little friend Terry, who sat at the same table as I did, put the wrong bits right and tied a perfect bow. Terry wore a bright blue knitted jersey and had a crew cut, evidently for economy, since for the rest of the term his ears and face slowly disappeared under a thatch of hair. I liked Terry, and he liked me, but I was revolted by the touch of his hairy leg against mine under the table.

We went outside to scream and play, came in and sat down silently with arms folded on the tables. Miss Farmer lifted the heavy blackboard onto its easel and picked up a chalk.

"I'm going to draw a picture. You tell me what it is."

She had a wooden box with coloured chalks, bright pink, blue, green, yellow, mauve, red, a rainbow of delight such as I had never seen. Chalking at home, for reasons I could well understand, was confined to white only. On the blackboard, in no time at all, appeared a splendid apple, half red and half green, with a stalk. How wonderfully clever grown-up people are! It looks real. Apples really are red and green. I can do that. I'll do it at home with crayons, but she's put the stalk in a funny place. I would put it at the top.

"What have I drawn, children?"

"An apple," came the chanted reply.

There must be some merit or magic in that strange, slow, declamatory mono-tone, I thought to myself. I will say it like that next time.

Since some children had been heard to say 'a apple', this had to be corrected before our studies could proceed.

"Apple starts with A, and A says 'a'. Say 'a'."

We did.

" 'a' for apple. Say it again."

Again we did.

"Now I'll rub out all the middle, and we are left with 'a'. Can you remember?"

The lovely apple, with its colouring-in rubbed out was now just a shape, but a shape invested with a deep scholarly significance. Miss Farmer proceeded to 'b' which began as a jolly blue balloon with a string, and was reduced by the wood and felt blackboard rubber to a skeleton of its former self.

Yes, I know what she's going to say. Balloon begins with a 'B', and that says 'b'. It's good! I like going to school. What will she draw next?

But that was it for the day. We were not expected to absorb more at a sitting than that. We were given little individual blackboards on which to draw the pictures and shapes, but not, of course, with coloured chalks.

At this rate of two letters a day it must have taken us about three weeks to cover the alphabet. It was then assumed that the class as a whole was ready for word-building. Number One chart came out on Monday morning. We were shown how two letters standing together made one sound, beginning, of course, with 'am', 'an', 'as', 'if', 'in', and so on through all the vowels. Miss Farmer took her long pointer in hand shaped like a billiard cue, and pointed to the first word, which we intoned in unison. Having taken us through all those words she turned back the huge, shiny page of Chart One to reveal Page two, on which was a gripping tale of an ox, with real sentences made from the words we had just learnt.

It is an ox. an ox is at us. is it in? is it on us?

an ox is at us. an ox is as it is. it is up. it is in.

In turning the page Miss Farmer had almost turned two by mistake, and I caught a glimpse of the next story. It had long words with three letters, which promised a better story line. I hoped we would have that one the next day.

"How do you like school then, Jane?" Daddy naturally wanted to know.
Silence.

"Aren't you going to tell us then? You were dying to get there and now you've got nothing to say."

I had plenty to say, but little about school. Never before had I had a life apart from the family, and I wanted to keep this separate life of mine quite private, without the intrusion of influences from home. It is a very common phenomenon among small children, sometimes hurtful to parents, but it is an initial reaction, and always eases out as the child learns to accept the duality of his new life as a normal state.

I soon gave up walking to and from school with Lucy and her friends, because now I had friends from my own class who went my way, Lily and Vera and Muriel. Vera had a long string of small brothers and sisters at home, which formed a link between us as we shared experiences and compared ages and stages.

Our mathematical education proceeded in a most orderly fashion. Miss Farmer taught us to recognise and write the figures, and to count by rote. Since the very first day I had been making conjectures about the possible uses of a tall stand in the corner of the room, on which was a large picture frame holding big coloured beads on wires. Ten beads in a row, I made it, and ten such rows. The moment arrived when Miss Farmer wheeled it out before the class and pushed all the beads along with a clatter to the left-hand side.

"Watch me count, children."

We watched, whilst she counted one line, moving the beads singly and slowly. She did it again. We were silent with expectation.

"Who can count like that for me?"

Elsie volunteered, and struggled through with help. Then Terry was chosen. With the supreme joy of privilege shining through his crew cut he began to count, moving several beads with each number he said, determined at all costs to move more beads to a count of ten than any other child in the class.

"Oh dear," said Miss Farmer, quite gently, "I don't think you were watching, Terry. Come on, Jane. I can see you are bursting to have a go."

I couldn't see Terry's problem, because Lucy had taught me to count, so I returned to my little armchair in a warm glow of intellectual achievement.

Our work in sums progressed daily and fast, at a rate dictated by the curriculum, which had been humanely designed for the average child, making no allowance for the really dull or the really bright.

CHAPTER FOUR

"What you got in that daft case?"

'Daft' was one of the two swear-words that Lucy and I knew. The other was 'fool'. They were never to be used in our home.

The speaker was May, one of Lucy's peers, but not of course a friend. We could not be friends with a girl who said 'daft'. She was a big girl for eight, and I was a little bit frightened by this sudden confrontation in Rockingham Road. There were some shaky knees a few inches below my hemline.

"My nightie." I told her, "And my clean vest and knickers. I'm going to my Grandma's for a little holiday."

"With that daft little case?" My adversary was a trifle short on adjectives.

"You have to have a real case to go on your holidays, and go on a train."

She skipped a few 'peppers' with her wooden-handled skipping-rope, an enviable possession. We each had a skipping-rope, sash-cord with a knot at either end.

"Well, I'm going to sleep there. And my sister."

I walked on, carrying my twelve-inch cardboard case with a great sense of occasion. May ran backwards to face me as I walked forwards, the more easily to taunt me.

"Where does your Grandma live then?"

I pointed up the road.

"That house with the green fence."

I was now about a quarter of a mile from home, and about thirty yards from the green fence, so I had no need to say, "My father's a policeman", which was the standard lie of the weaker faction. I walked on, opened the gate, went in and shut it, turning often to see if May was still following. But she was standing outside the gate, gazing after me with something very like envy, and chewing the round bit of her skipping-rope handle. I approached the front door as an official visitor and stretched on my toes to grasp the bell-pull, a large, pear-shaped object, hollow, with decorative perforations, which would certainly by now be a valuable antique. The inside bell made a gratifying tintinabulation in the passage and brought Grandma to the door, kind and aristocratic-looking in her pinc-nez.

"Hello, darling. Where's Lucy then?"

"She's gone to the anniversary practice at Sunday school, and she's coming at half-past seven." This was Friday evening, special practice night, but not for the little ones.

We went up stairs to the bedroom which we were to use. Grandma had plenty of spare bedrooms now. All her children had left home, except the youngest, a boy of fourteen who went to Christ's Hospital, and was only home for the holidays.

I did the unpacking, having brought Lucy's things as well as my own. I was secretly disappointed to find that we were to share a bed, as we now had to do at home.

"How's Mamma, dear? Is she all right?"

Such questions, which were often asked, always aroused my niggling anxieties. My stout denials of any health problems at home were in reality me reassuring myself. We had long been promised this little holiday, "sometime in the summer", and now, suddenly, it had come. No shared bed, or shadows of worry were going to spoil it for me.

Lucy arrived, hot with running and excitement, and we were allowed a little while to play in the garden. It was a tiny garden with a small soft-fruit patch, a tiny little lawn surrounded by borders with a few forget-me-nots and pansies. We were quite familiar with it, but this time it had a fresh glamour, because we were visitors on our own, staying a few days.

Half-past eight was very late for our bed-time, but it was a holiday and Grandma took liberties with the clock. She gave us bread and butter and milk for supper before taking us up the stairs and tucking us up in the double bed.

"I wonder if Uncle William used to wet this bed," Lucy suggested with a giggle.

"That's rude," I said, strong in defence of virtue. "Anyway, how do you know this was Uncle William's room? It might have been Auntie Jane's."

"Can't you smell the tobacco on the eiderdown? Auntie Jane doesn't smoke. Ladies aren't allowed to."

"I saw a lady smoking a cigarette the other day. She was taking her dog for a walk."

"Well, anyhow, all these books are Uncle William's. He's written his name in them."

She jumped out of bed and got one. I followed and got another, and sure enough, Uncle William's name was written on the fly leaf.

"Don't be silly. You can't read joined-up writing. You can't read properly at all yet."

"Yes, I can. I'll read this."

The book was 'Tanglewood Tales' by Nathaniel Hawthorne, my first incursion into Greek mythology. Most of the words were already familiar to me, and the strange and difficult names I broke open with a phonic sledge-hammer. Lucy was impressed. Sheepishly she felt around for her favourite lock of hair and twisted it round her finger, then put it in her mouth.

"Actually," she conceded, "you're quite a good reader for five."

The room seemed full of drawers and cupboards, none full, and none completely empty. We were soon busily exploring them, with only a faint sense of naughtiness. My conscience was trying to make an observation, but I was relying on Lucy's conscience to make the decisions, and it seemed to be suffering no discomfort. We found collar studs, safety pins, playing cards and postcards, pencil stubs and some small, sealed rubber containers which mystified us both. (We later found out that they were capsules of lighter fuel.) Drawer by drawer we learned more of our Uncle William, putting everything back where it belonged before moving on to the next. Suddenly, of course, the door opened, and we were caught in the act.

"What are you little girls doing? You should have been asleep hours ago."

We leapt guiltily into bed and waited for the moral bit.

"It's not quite polite to look in other people's drawers, is it? I'm sure you know that."

"Sorry, Grandma." Lucy was nearly in tears.

"All right, darling. I expect you both got a little bit excited. Let me tuck you in, and then you must go to sleep."

The next day was Saturday, so we had a long time to spend in that tiny garden. There were no toys, and none of our friends lived near. There was a water-butt, and by standing on tiptoe we could see into it. The water looked deep, dark and threatening, and the surface was covered with small jerking, swimming creatures. We tried to catch some with leaves from the Virginia creeper which was blushing modestly all over the outside toilet. I took a deep dislike to these water-skimmers,

13

not of course knowing that they were mosquito larvae. The shoots of the red-leaved creeper provided another amusement, as they grow first upwards and then bend over, giving the whole plant the appearance of burgeoning with small green swans. We picked them and tried to float them in the water-butt, where of course they fell sideways, sad little green swans without hope.

In the afternoon, her work finished, Grandma took us to play in Greenham Park. In 1924 this was a much bigger park, the grounds of the old house which has served as a school clinic, dental clinic, and baby clinic for so many years. Recently restored, it is now fulfilling its purpose as a family day centre run by the National Childrens' Homes.

Lucy and I sometimes went on our own to play in Greenham Park, long before any swings and slides had been installed. Our excitement on these occasions was greatly heightened by the legend of 'the Keeper', a terrifying authority figure whose purpose in life was to catch naughty children. Let any bold little fellow put so much as one toe where it said, 'keep off the grass', and he would be quickly surrounded by pale-faced children breathing "Look out! The keeper'll see you!"

In the event we never saw the keeper. Very likely, as with Kafka's Castle, there was no-one there.

I began to get homesick by the second bed-time and asked when we were going back.

"No, not tomorrow, dear. After school on Monday you can go home in time for tea."

I needed my mother desparately by then and was glad when our little holiday was over. We called at Grandma's house after school to collect our attache case and ran home eagerly.

Nurse Hawdon had done it again! There was a little new sister, very red and crumply, crying, and as always, entirely unexpected.

"Now we've got five," I announced triumphantly. "We've got as many as Vera."

We were kept in complete ignorance of the facts of life, with regard to the basics of sex and reproduction until the imparted knowledge of older children made rents in our innocence. Our parents told us no lies. Storks and gooseberry bushes and little black bags formed no part of our creed, but we were also told none of the truth.

CHAPTER FIVE

Our next holiday was a far grander affair, two years later. We were seated around the breakfast table, having consumed our cocoa, bread and butter and half a banana each when Mamma said significantly,

"Now listen. I have something to tell you."

It sounded promising. We were all agog.

"Daddy has done rather well with his camera this year and won some good prizes, so we're going to take you all to the seaside for a few days, and I expect we shall stay for a week."

This mention of a few days, followed by the promise of a week, was strange, but they were her exact words. If she intended in this way to break it gently to us and thus to moderate our excitement, she failed. We shouted, and left our places to jump up and down in a perfect heaven of anticipation.

We were to go to Salcombe, in South Devon, my father's home town, where his parents still lived. Grandpa had been the manager of the gas works, and we had once before spent a short time in the big house near the gas-holder. My recollection is of a rather gloomy house with two staircases leading from the hall and meeting to form a little gallery. The garden was wild and interesting, and the gas-holder itself, floating on its tank of water was terrifyingly attractive. We had been taken to the beach and to South Sands, where we played and paddled in a little stream which ran over the sand to the sea, and on which we picked up pearly shells. Lucy and I had disgraced ourselves on this holiday by setting out to find the sea, which Lucy was sure she could see from the back garden. Unfortunately, what she had seen through the hedge was a muddy backwater, and by the time we had realised our mistake we were coated from head to foot in black, slimy mud.

This time it was to be different. Grandpa had retired from work and he and Grandma were building a bungalow on a large tract of land which he had bought. They were literally building it, with their own four hands and very little other help.

"It is not quite finished yet," Mamma told us, "so you mustn't mind if the walls are still a bit rough."

We did not mind anything. We were going to the seaside. The little ones had not seen the sea, or could not remember it. The red, crumply baby had turned into my small sister Doreen, a sweet, serious little girl of nearly two. I longed to introduce her to the delights of the seaside. The age-gap of six years allowed me to appreciate her as a baby, attractive and adorable. I was motherly towards her.

The train journey itself was excitement enough. For a little while we sat, still and virtuous, on the red plush seats, until the harshness of the material began to irritate the bare skin under our knees. Then we sidled out into the corridor and found much to interest us in gazing through the window. As we passed through Dawlish I shouted for all to hear,

"We're there. I can see the sea!"

I could. It was washing up under the train wheels. But we were still a long way from our destination.

We changed trains onto a small branch line for Kingsbridge, and it was dark when we reached there. Tired and confused we were bundled into a taxi by a strange aunt who had come to meet us. This was my father's older sister Anne, who kept a fruit shop in Salcombe, a big, kindly woman who gave us a banana each to eat in the taxi. We were hungry and appreciative.

"My! You made short work of that one! Would you like another?"

I accepted, and made equally short work of it. Never before had we had such an opportunity.

There were nine of us in the taxi, with the little ones all on adult knees. The driver pulled up at a dark corner and opened the door.

"Can't go no further, Ma'am."

"Oh, Jack, surely, with all these little ones? You're never going to drop us here?"

"I wouldn't take my cab down there in daylight, Ma'am, let alone at night. Sorry about the babies."

So we all got out and walked. Mamma and Daddy carried Norma and Doreen, Peter whimpered and walked, whilst Lucy and I helped Auntie Anne to carry the luggage. On the way down the lane Lucy whispered to me,

"This is corn. I can feel it. We shan't have anywhere to play."

It was not very far to the new bungalow, which certainly did look a bit depressing to the exhausted travellers. The dim light from several small paraffin lamps made eerie shadows on the brise-block walls and the bare floor. We had some supper and were taken off to bed, where further to my distress I found that we were to sleep on the floor. The little girls were already asleep, and Peter was crying with homesickness. As we crept into our rough blanket Lucy confided her fear about the corn.

"Don't you worry, my dear. You'll have plenty of room to play." Our floor-bed was, in the event, quite comfortable, and we soon fell asleep.

Inevitably we woke early, so Lucy and I dressed and went out. In the daylight we could see the delightful position of the bungalow, the flight of rough-hewn steps leading down to a path through the woods, the wide areas of rough ground covered with grass and wild flowers, the steep bank behind the house, and the lane we had walked in last night. We solved the riddle of the corn too. The lane was bordered with pink and white campions, ox-eye daisies, and a kind of grass which we called wild oats. It was these which Lucy had felt in the dark. Standing on the ridge of Grandpa's land we looked down the slope towards the wood and saw a sight so wonderful that we doubted our eyes. Wild apples! Red ones and yellow ones, big and small, all growing on trees old and half-choked with rank grass and weeds. We bounded down the slope and gathered all we could carry, then went back up to the house to tell Grandpa about the wonderful unknown resources we had discovered for him on his new land.

But it was Grandma we met, practical, prudent, unimaginative Devonshire Grandma.

"Oh, lor! You haven't bin picking them apples? That is naughty! Look, these are keepers, and you don't want to pick them till they're ripe enough to store. I'll see you gets apples t'eat. You've no call to go picking them off the trees."

I was a little afraid of Devonshire Grandma. She had a kind enough heart, but a sharp critical tongue, with which no doubt she had kept her own large family in order. Grandpa, in contrast, was a gently-spoken man, sensitive and understanding towards everyone.

Seeing how our good intentions had brought us embarrassment and shame on the very first morning he said,

"Come out with me, my dears, and I'll show you the sea."

He lifted his cap from the back of the door by its peak and used both hands to settle it on his head. Then he gave us each a hand and led us round to the front of the bungalow.

"Now you stand up there, my little love," he said, lifting me onto the wooden seat he had made for that spot, "and you get up alongside, little maid. Now look, there's the sea."

He pointed over the field and the tops of the trees, but all I could see was sky. "Don't you see it? 'Tis out there, look, right over yon."

Lucy could see it, but I could not. I just saw sky, pale blue and gold. And then a little sailing ship moved into this sky, which helped me to adjust my perception. Then I could make out both sea and sky, meeting on the horizon.

"Where's the sand?" I wanted to know.

"You can't see it from here. It's too far away. The sand's there alright."

We jumped off the wooden seat, climbed up again and jumped off again, until Mamma called us into the tent. Since the bathroom and toilet were not yet finished a tent had been erected at the side of the bungalow. Here we washed in enamel bowls and sat on little potties with our bare feet on the grass, while the canvas walls flapped in and out. Hygiene was not our responsibility. We were joyously carefree.

At last we were ready for the beach, sandwiches made and packed, buckets and spades tied together through the handles, Daddy's camera and photographic plates laid ready in a safe place.

It was this very camera which had given us our holiday. My father was an imaginative and artistic photographer, in the days when knowledge, skill and experience were needed for good results. There were no automatic aids. Distances had to be measured out, or calculated, light was a matter of observation and judgment, shutter-speed had to be set by hand and according to experience, for flashlight pictures the flashpowder had to be mixed, then sparked off by a flint. My father had made a name for himself locally, and had won several big prizes in nation-wide competitions. Most of his work was studies of children, but he also had a wonderful eye for out-door subjects, ploughing horses, birds, primroses, sea and landscapes. While we were very young we did not mind being endlessly photographed, but we grew to dislike it as we became older.

Sunday evening was a favourite time for him to take pictures of his children engaged in a variety of pursuits. He was a most inventive picture-maker, and we were recorded posed on stools, with and without clothes, reading to each other, painting, playing schools even standing on our heads against the door with our skirts about our faces. Out of doors he found even more opportunities.

Sunday evening was special in two ways. It was the time of the weekly story, a never-ending serial invented and told by myself, and the time for camera work, involving us all. It became a tradition for one of us, as tea drew to a close, to set up the chant of 'Story night. Picture night!' and all would join in. The story filled up the boring time which was needed for Daddy to set up the camera on a stand, a bed sheet to act as a reflector, a piece of white tissue paper to diffuse the flash. The flashgun itself, home-made from a tin, had to be fed with home-made flashpowder. The room had to be cleared, and various chairs and stools set ready. Then came the moment for getting the children posed. We hated this part, and wriggled and complained, but Daddy was always patient and usually promised us a little reward for when it was over. I had to have my back to the camera, because the flash always made be blink, and the exposures at that time were not fast enough to miss this.

When all was set up Daddy would say, "Ready now", and manually remove the cap to expose the lens. Simultaneously he had to trigger the flash and immediately replace the lens cap. It required the dexterity of a juggler and the concentration of a judge. The climax for us came when the flash ignited the tissue paper, as it invariably did, and we, now free from pose, would make a rush to stamp on it and catch the flying bits. We were duly rewarded with half an apple for our supper. They were great days.

Salcombe, with its wonderful cliff walks and rock formations surrounded by foaming water is a photographer's paradise. Whilst we were playing on the beach Daddy would walk around, weighed down with heavy equipment, and take some of the loveliest pictures I have ever seen.

Devonshire Grandpa had a boat, quite a big one, with an outboard motor. He had made it himself and called it the 'Elizabeth Anne' after his wife. He took us all for trips in this boat, which enabled us to visit other beaches, Millbay and Sunny Cove, instead of being confined to South Sands, which was within walking distance. Returning one evening in the boat Mamma picked up little Doreen and held her over the side with her feet trailing in the water, which was very deep and very still.

"Don't, Mamma, Don't!" I shrieked.

She took no notice as Doreen was enjoying it.

"You'll drop her, Mamma. She'll sink down. Bring her in!"

I was getting hysterical and near to tears, so my plea was granted and the baby was saved from the horrors of the deep.

The unfinished bungalow was our home for the whole sunny week, and we loved it. It was a sad day when we had to leave. In the train going home I was oppressed by a sense of the passing of time. It had been an iridescent, classic, standard-setting sort of holiday, the last we were to have as a complete family.

CHAPTER SIX

Both my parents came from Methodist families, so although neither of them was deeply religious it was natural for them to send us to the Methodist Sunday School. The primitive Methodist church was at our end of the town, on the site now occupied by insurance offices, a travel agency, and other businesses. But we were Wesleyan Methodists, and between us and the 'Prims' there was in those days a wide gulf fixed. Like most people, we had no car, and this meant a long walk of a mile and a half each way for Lucy and me. We were regular in attendance, not only from parental conviction I think, but also because it was the only time that Mamma and Daddy had together. I used to be quite bewildered on getting home to find them doing absolutely nothing in two armchairs.

The Primary department was run by Mrs. Smith, a gentle-looking person with very white hair. There were two long semicircles of children, interspersed with pretty young teachers, and after a few little songs and prayers we formed circles of chairs, each with one of the pretty teachers, to listen to a story. These stories were not so good as the ones at day school, but any story was a joy.

When the story was over we replaced the chairs and had what Mrs. Smith called a 'march round'. Miss Mooney at the piano gave a brisk rendering of 'The Soldiers' March', whilst we circumnavigated the two rows of chairs. This would have been great fun if only the children would have marched properly, but they merely drifted slowly round the chairs regardless of Miss Mooney's bright staccato.

We did a good deal of singing, which I liked. Mrs. Smith asked me if I would sing 'Little beam of rosy light' for the anniversary the following week, and I agreed, so we ran through it for practice. Unfortunately the book she lent me was the music copy, and I got hopelessly confused because all the first lines of the verses were printed under the first line of the music.

It was a great privilege to take the collection. Since there were about fifty children in the Primary department it was a privilege which did not come very often. Our collecting box was most unusual, a square glass box with a wooden handle and we could see our pennies dropping into it. Miss Mooney would desert her piano during story time to empty this box and count the money. It was some time before Lucy told me that the money was not for her.

During the collection we used to sing,

> 'Hear the pennies dropping
> Listen while they fall.
> Every one for Jesus,
> He shall have them all.' . . .

. . . but I, having in mind the attractive display of Goudas outside the International Stores, was singing,

> 'Every one for cheeses.'

This particular anniversary was the one in which I was to perform my solo at the afternoon service. Unfortunately on the walk down I lost my collection penny, and we spent a long time hunting for it among the dock and nettles of the allotments in Craven Road, a site now occupied by the pensioners' flatlets. To leave it there was unthinkable. It represented a whole week's pocket money, but we were

19

obliged at last to abandon the search and hasten on. Upon arrival I was immediately grabbed by the wrist and pushed up the steps onto the stage to face a hall full of parents and children. Panting and disshevelled and hot from the street I sailed into my number -

> 'Little beam of rosy light,
> Who has made you shine so bright?
> 'Tis our Fa - a - ther,
> 'Tis our Father.

> Little bird with golden wing,
> Who has taught you how to sing?
> 'Tis our Father,
> 'Tis our Father.

Then with a complete change of tempo which I always loved,

> 'Tis our Father God above,
> He has made us, he is love.'

"Thank you Jane." said Mrs. Smith. "I was afraid you weren't coming."
"Well, I lost my penny."
"And did you find it?"
"No." this was the best part of the performance for the audience.
"Well, as you sang so nicely for us I daresay we can find you another."
She helped me down off the platform to a gratifying roar of applause, the applause given to a performance completed against heavy odds.

That evening we walked down to the church for yet a third time, but this time the older boys and girls, which included Lucy, sat in the back gallery, Auntie Edith had come with me and we sat in the side gallery together. The bigger children sang songs and recited verses, and then our superintendent called upon the special speaker to give us his address. This nice gentleman forgot to tell us where he lived, but he soon captured all attention by producing an enormous pencil, about a yard long and correspondingly thick.

"Not real." Lucy told me afterwards, with her shattering sceptism.

Life, our speaker told us, was like a clean page on which we could write, and we should try to write without making mistakes. But if we had made a mistake, (he now produced an enormous rubber, cardboard, according to Lucy,) we could rub it out and begin again with a clean page. And what is our eraser? God's forgiveness, of course, which allows us to make a fresh start. The aptness of this illustration appealed to me immensely. I had had a good day.

At this stage I was puzzled by the nature of God. There seemed to be two Gods. There was the God of Sunday School, who was kind and gentle and loved little children, and there was Miss Chilvers' God, who lived in the Ark, (not Noah's Ark, but the Ark of the Covenant), whose divine objective seemed to be, like the keeper's, to catch naughty children. I had been promoted now to the second class of the Infant School, and Miss Chilvers was my new teacher. Since in each case God was said to be three in one my infant arithmetic made six of them. The Sunday School God was the father of that baby Jesus, and was invisible and therefore unknowable, but people really had seen Jesus when he had lived on earth, so it was possible, it seemed, to address our prayers to him, and he would pass on the message.

Miss Chilvers' God was also invisible, even if you looked inside the Ark, and he was the God who said 'Thou shalt not'. We were on no account, for instance, to covet our neighbour's ox, nor his ass, nor his maid-servant nor his man-servant. The ox, I find, was quite a feature of my early education. Its influence upon my subsequent life has been minimal. The people next door had none of these possessions, so I was not sorely tempted to covetousness. Stealing was of course, and killing your neighbour not recommended. 'Thou shalt not commit adultery' was not explained by Miss Chilvers, so I asked my father.

"Daddy, what's adultery?"

Something flickered a moment behind his eyes but he recovered quickly. "It's when something bad is mixed with something good, and spoils it, like, . . ." he brightened considerably at the recollection, "like on the flour bags, it says, 'PURE AND UNADULTERATED'."

"Well, what does God want us not to mix up?"

"Ah, well, when you're young it's hard to understand some things like that. You will later on."

There was a noticeable lack of entente between day school and Sunday School teaching. I sought desparately for a compromise.

The only times we missed Sunday School were on the infrequent occasions when we were ill, and once or twice in the summer when we went to Enborne for a picnic. The Sunday School teachers understood this reason for absence, and were sympathetic towards it. Not so Miss Chilvers.

Each Monday morning there was a lesson called 'conversation'. As an ideal it was good, but on the practical level it was a little ambitious to try to make good conversationalists out of fifty inhibited five-year-olds in half an hour a week. Miss Chilvers method was to work round her class in strict order, expecting each child to stand up and deliver one complete sentence, then sit down. On this day we all had to begin our sentence with 'Yesterday I . . .'.

It was a riveting conversation. "Stand up." "Yesterday I went to my Granny's." "Sit down." "Stand up." "Yesterday I wore my new shoes." "Sit down." "Stand up." "Yesterday I got up late." "Sit down."

My turn came. "Stand up."

"Yesterday we went for a picnic at Enborne."

"It's wicked to go for picnics on Sundays. Sit down."

It was like a punch in the solar plexus. I would have sat down anyway. Wicked! But Mamma and Daddy took us. We were all so happy. I know teachers are always right, but Mamma and Daddy aren't wicked. We weren't working on the Sabbath, only playing. Actually Mamma did cut the sandwiches and make the lemonade. Perhaps she is a little wicked. I hope God won't do that thing Miss Chilvers told us about to Mamma.

I was worried all the morning, and while we were eating our dinner at home I timidly ventured,

"Miss Chilvers said it's wicked to go for picnics on Sundays."

"Oh, she did, did she?" There was an edge to my mother's voice.

"She says everything's wicked," thus Lucy.

"Is it, Mamma?" I was longing for an explanation.

"No, of course not, but perhaps her own parents taught her that, so of course she believes it."

She evidently told our father, because when he came up to say goodnight to us that evening he said,

"If I were you, Jane, I should take more notice of the Sunday School teachers about right and wrong. Mind you, the school teachers know more about learning, so you listen to what they tell you." I knew just what he meant. I was slowly reaching that conclusion myself through other channels.

CHAPTER SEVEN

Having romped happily through Infant School I found myself, at six years old, in Standard One of the big school. Now once again I was passing the day in the same building as Lucy, and could experience for myself the exciting high life and the high risks of which she so often told me. Here we had reading books with proper stories in them. No more waiting for all the children to battle with -

"Ned had a bun. It was a jam bun.

It was in his cap, but he did not see it.

He put his cap on. Ha. Ha. The jam was on Ned."

Nor more smacks for losing the place through feasting on the frugal delights of the last page whilst the class and teacher were stuck at 'the place' along with the slowest reader. Now we were reading 'The Fairy Queen', (bright blue), and 'The Cuckoo Clock' by Mrs. Molesworth, (bright red), which told the sad tale of little Griselda who thought the buns contained too much cinnamon, and whose little friend Paul wore a velvet suit which he called his 'welpet'. Here, too, we learned about verbs and nouns, pounds, shillings and pence, foreign lands and olden times. Cedric the Saxon and Marcus the Roman opened up for me splendid prospects of more exciting and seemingly endless things to learn about. We also learned to sing tunes from tonic solfa, both chart and hand-sign, springing into action at the ping of a tuning fork.

There were troubles of course. On our first day we were given a pen-holder and a nib to push into it. That done we were shown how to dip the nib in the inkwell, (those mysterious holes explained at last), and how to make the down strokes heavy and the up strokes light. That was it. Very simple to an adult. But my nib quickly developed a will of its own and became an enemy, digging into the paper and splattering ink over my fresh exercise book like newsprint. Because of my struggles with the ink my progress was slow, and I soon gained the reputation of being 'all behind, like the donkey's tail'. I had to stay in while the others went out to play, to catch up, and all because of my recalcitrant nib. I was a fluent writer with a pencil, but we had to master the pen.

A further indignity awaited me. We were allowed to use pencils for sums for a week or two, and the giving-out monitress had the privilege of distributing them to the seated children. As the pencils were always in various stages of chewed-upness the monitress took good care to save herself the longest. As she drew along-side my dual desk, and was choosing me a nice one because I was her friend the teacher sang out -

"Give Jane a small one. She's got such little hands."

That set the pattern for all future givers-out of pencils. They were the privileged class, these monitresses. Now that we were in the big school the boys had been hived off, so it was many years before I realised that there could also be monitors.

We had monitresses of all kinds. Our teachers kept great state. There was teacher's monitress, the greatly favoured, who carried the sacred books and bag from staffroom to classroom and back, the door monitress, whose onerous task it was to open the door before her and close it after her. This office carried the high privilege of being allowed to hang on to the door-knob possessively during the long moments of waiting. There was the blackboard monitress, to clean the board upon request, and to beat out the chalk from the rubber by banging it for dear life on the outside wall, producing a sandstorm of dust and some satisfying designs on the brickwork. The flower monitress had the joy of staying in on sunny playtimes to wash out slimy, green jam-jars to accommodate the sticky buds. There was even competition for the job of lavatory monitress, a post which carried the heavy responsibility of standing all playtime at the entrance to the long row of loos to write down the names of any children caught 'playing about', or whom she did not like.

Of course these toilets were not without their temptation. In order to avoid a freeze-up in frosty weather each lavatory pan had been hemmed in by a wooden retaining board across the front, and completely surrounded by sawdust. As far as I can remember it achieved its object perfectly, but sawdust is an attractive continuous-quantity material for young children to play with, and tossing was not unknown. Hence the need for total monitress cover. I could not leave it alone. I used to sit on the seat, burying a hand in the little bran tub on either side, but the only treasures to be retrieved were empty sherbet-fountain tubes, orange peel, apple cores and paper bags with names on them.

Knitting and needlework caused me a certain amount of trouble, because I was only six at the time, and we were learning plain and pearl ribbing, and hemming. I could knit at home where I only did plain stitches, and no-one minded if my rows grew longer by arithmetical progression. But the girls at school laughed at my efforts.

The hemming was learned on a practice piece, white turning to grey with the passing of time. Once a girl had mastered the difficult business of picking up a bit from the bottom and a bit from the top of her hem she progressed to the making of a teatowel. This was sewing for real, and I longed to do it, but had not yet qualified. One afternoon the teacher got seated among her needles and reels and said,

"All the girls with teatowels come to me."

All the girls with teatowels leapt up and formed a line by her desk, self-conscious, elect, and trying to look modest. I had run out of cotton for my practice piece so I joined the queue.

The teacher cast an eye along the line.

"That's a very small teatowel you have, Jane."

I realised my mistake, and slunk back to my desk, followed by titters, a very small teatowel with a very small owner.

When it came to knitting on four needles in the next term the hands which were too small for a long pencil earned me no sympathy.

"Whatever will you do when you get married, and your husband wants socks?" Laughter in the class.

From time to time we were visited in class by the school nurse. She was a massive woman, dressed in purple, both long and wide, with a purple veil worn over her head and floating out behind her like a banner.

When she sailed into the classrooms we knew she was on a nit-hunt, with her little glass stick and tweezers. Our class teacher would retreat to a position behind the blackboard with a notebook and pencil in the fond hope that none of us could see when she was writing down a name. We all knew who had what.

But one day, to my blushing humiliation, my name was written down, not for nits, but because I had a touch of eczema behind my ear. The next morning a big girl was sent to our class to fetch me, and all unknown to my mother I was taken to the school clinic in Greenham House.

The big girl and I walked up the brown lino-covered stairs and into the room marked 'Clinic'. There, large and purple as ever, was Nitty Nora. She bathed my ear and applied some pink ointment, then covered her work with a strip of lint.

"Tell your mother she's not to take it off, and come again on Thursday."

At dinner time I went home and explained what had happened.

"You're not to take it off, the nurse said."

"Did she indeed! Well, really!" Her tone implied what I had felt. Free treatment for school children did not include common courtesy.

I did not have to attend the clinic many times, as the condition soon cleared up, but after that I always felt sympathy for those who had their names written down.

The few drawbacks of being in the big school were well compensated. Our geography lessons were made very exciting by models, for which we brought the materials, and which our teacher assembled. They were strictly 'look but don't touch' models, about two feet by eighteen inches. The first was an arctic landscape with white paper mountains and lumps of washing soda for the ice-bergs. We moved from below zero to the high tropics and made a model of an Amazon jungle, paper trees festooned with paper flowers and horrendous snakes of glitter wax. Strewn sand with cardboard pyramids made by teacher was the desert, crossed by caravans of sandy plasticine camels. Crude, small models they may have been, with the minimum of child participation in the making, yet imagination made them glow with all the romance of foreign travel.

In the Summer term there was swimming for the children in the big school. On Wednesday afternoon every one turned up with a costume and a rubber cap rolled up in a towel, all of which were stowed under our pegs until half-past two. Then the children lined up at the classroom door in a crocodile, which remained unbroken until we reached the dressing boxes, a walk of about a mile.

The baths, as we called them, were in the same spot as now, but were far more primitive. There was the 'duck's pond' for little children, and the big water for the others, and the mechanics of water supply were the same for both, simply a couple of inlets where the river could enter. With the water came tadpoles, minnows, algae, small pieces of river weeds, so the swimming pools were really just captured bits of river, but stagnant instead of running. Spirogyra coated the bottom and sides of the bath with green slime, which grew upwards through its native element, so that at times one was swimming through a clinging green web, on equal terms with the fish and the tadpoles. But it seemed good value to us, at a penny for as long as you liked.

School swimming was free, but of course we had only a few minutes in the water, as many classes from all the schools needed the facilities. So we had to get in quickly, no matter how cold it was, and 'duck' at once by order. Then we were allowed to play about and pretend to swim, whilst the neatly-dressed teacher on the brink gave us each a turn on the rope. This was a halter which we put over our heads and under our arms, standing a yard or two out to sea. We were then commanded to take our feet off the bottom and were hauled to the side, threshing at random with all four limbs. Thus most of us learnt to swim.

Lily, Vera, Muriel and I used to share a dressing-box if we could get one of the large ones. There we would stand, talking and shivering, too cold to get dressed.

"My Mum says I've got a well-shaped body. Do you think I've got a well-shaped body?"

Lily had at last towelled herself dry, and now turned round in her little private patch of water to give us a chance to judge. She had all four limbs in good working order, and I did not know what other criteria to apply.

"Yes, you have." Vera and I agreed.

"Do you think I have?" I turned my naked self around.

"Oh, yes, you have. You're well-built."

I cogitated upon this verbal distinction. Well-shaped, or well-built? Perhaps the latter meant the same as sturdy, which was what Newbury Grandma called me. Like Lily I had four well-rounded limbs and plenty of energy, all that an eight-year-old needs.

During the Summer holidays Lucy and I spent many happy hours amongst the minnows and spirogyra. Most of our friends would congregate there too, and the time flew by as we shouted and splashed. One afternoon as we were leaving with our wet bundles under our arms the 'man' shouted after us some-what rudely,

" 'Ad yer pennyworth, ain't yer?"

Our parents were very interested in our education, and supportive in every way they knew while we were small. It was in the later stages of my schooling that I was aware of a lack of support, not through any unkindness, but from sheer non-understanding of higher education, of its needs and its opportunities.

I was doing my homework, as the 'scholarship children' did every evening in preparation for the February examination.

"What's nine eights, Daddy?"

"Seventy-two. But oughtn't you to know that if you're doing those sums?"

"Well, I missed all the hard tables. They learned them in Standard Two."

I had 'jumped' from Standard One to Standard Three, and later from four to six.

Daddy put a hand in his pocket and drew out his purse, the kind with a little tray into which you tip the coins and select what you need.

"Here you are, my dear, twopence. You can go down to Harrison's and buy a table book, then learn them."

I hurried off to the shop, delighted with this unexpected gift. It was only ten minutes walk away. 'Supa-News' now has a stationer's shop on the same premises. Proudly I carried home my newest treasure, 'Nuttall's Book of Tables'. Our dictionary was a Nuttall's, so I had complete confidence in the tables being right. That night I took it up to bed with me, and soon caught up with what I had missed.

Our parents found another way to help us. One afternoon a large parcel arrived at our house, addressed to Daddy, but as he was at work Mamma started to open it.

"I know what's in it," she said. "I think you will be interested."

We gathered round expectantly. It was a big cardboard box, and immensely heavy. The string came off and the papers, and both were saved, then the box was opened, revealing two piles of books, eight altogether.

We could not believe our eyes. They were big, heavy and new.

"Are they story books, Mamma?"

"Not exactly. They are encyclopedias, but there are stories in them."

They were 'The Cassell's Books of Knowledge', full of pictures, some of them coloured.

Before touching any of them Mamma made us all wash our hands and sit at the table. Then we were given one each to leaf through. We became very excited and shouted to each other about our individual discoveries.

"Can we read them whenever we like?" I asked.

"You must ask Daddy or me if you want one, and sit up to the table with it, as they are very heavy books, and very expensive. Would you like me to read one of the stories, so that the little ones can enjoy it?"

She sat on a Windsor chair by the lace-curtained window, and we fetched our small chairs and stools. The story she chose was about a monkey who found an apple in a bottle and put his paw in to get it. He could not get his paw out again because he was holding the apple and would not let go. He held on for days until the apple shrivelled up, and he was able to get it out, unfit to eat.

"Next time, Mamma, read us about how the soap bubble gets its colours, will you?"

"Perhaps."

Many happy hours were spent in perusing those encyclopedias, and many knotty problems solved by reference to them. The complete set is still in the family, much of its knowledge now outdated, or known to be incorrect.

CHAPTER EIGHT

It was Springtime, and Daddy was developing his negatives. He had adapted our bathroom as a darkroom, a fact which bothered us not at all as small children, but which was to give rise to friction and resentment as we grew older.

A moveable worktop had been laid across the bath, raised to a convenient working height. On this was a paraffin lamp in a stoutly-made wooden box with a sliding front door of red glass, producing the ghastly red light in which negatives were developed. The window was blacked out by a wooden frame, quite simple to insert and remove. The wash-basin was permanently out of commission, being filled with bottles and jars. Wooden shelving round the walls, and a cupboard with another working surface had all been produced in the garden shed to hold the great variety of chemicals and materials needed for the work. There was a strong aroma of paraffin lamp, bromide and general stuffiness, since the blacked out window could not be opened. I hated the smells and lack of air, but we were in any case not allowed in the darkroom at all when Daddy was working there, as even the faintest trace of daylight would have ruined the processing.

This evening in April he had finished developing his negatives, glass plates covered with sensitive film, and was washing them in a wax-lined wooden box he had made for the purpose, which stood in the kitchen sink. A treacle tin had been adapted by piercing a hole in the bottom and soldering in a bent length of lead piping. A wire fixed on the tin allowed it to hang over the tap and enclose the spout. A carefully adjusted stream of water was set running down the pipe into the tank containing the negatives, and entered with a 'glump-glump' sound which was a part of our infant environment. As clean water entered the floor of the tank, the dirty water needed draining off from the top, so another short length of lead pipe sat on the edge, swan-shaped, and performed this duty. It was all pure Heath Robinson, and totally effective.

"What are they, Daddy? When did you take them?"

"Primroses. You know when I went out yesterday on my bike. That's when I took them. When they're clean I'll let you see."

"They look perfectly clean to me." I said. "The water's all as clear as anything."

"Yes, but they have to be chemically clean, and that takes time. They're not dirty, but you have to allow time to wash all traces of chemicals out of them."

"What happens if you don't?"

"Well, then your pictures might fade, or go cloudy, in patches, which is worse."

I gazed down into the bubbling water, but could make out nothing yet. We were quite used to looking at negatives and making the necessary adjustments of perception, but until they were held up to the light there was nothing to see at all.

Daddy fetched his drying rack and hung it up in readiness. Then he turned off the tap and removed the tin.

"Now let's see what we've got."

He rather liked an audience at this moment. Like a magician at the climax of a trick he rubbed the untreated back of the glass plate with his hand and looked at it.

"Beautiful!" he said, "perfect. Have a look."

We were never allowed to touch the slides as the wet film was very delicate, so he held it for me to see.

"I thought primroses grew all over, you know, like daisies. Do they always grow like that, in a ring of leaves?"

"Well, you know, don't you? You've seen primroses growing."

"Not in the wood, I haven't. Only in people's gardens."

It was true. Our picnics were always in a field, or on the common.

"Go to the toilet and get your coat on. We'll go now."

He placed the precious plates in the drying rack and went to get his bicycle from the shed. He tied a cushion round the cross-bar, and attached the little stirrups he had made for the use of Peter, whom he often took for rides. Then we were off, on a trip made doubly exciting by being entirely unexpected.

We sped along the Enborne Road, past our picnic place, and on to the Craven Arms where we turned right. I cannot remember the other twists and turns by which we eventually arrived at Daddy's primrose wood. He unhitched me first, then lifted his bike over the gate and wheeled it out of sight.

"We can't come in here, Daddy. It says 'Trespassers will be prosecuted'."

"Don't you worry about that, my dear. We shan't do the least little bit of harm, and primroses grow for everyone to see."

Reassured I ran on into the little covert, and there they were, growing free and unravaged amongst the dog's mercury, wood anemones, and dead beech leaves. I did not pick them, or tread on them, but knelt on the moss to put my face into the living clumps, and I knew then that the look and the scent and the feel of primroses are three in one.

We could not stop long; it was only April and the evenings were still short, so we remounted our dual steed and made for home. It had been my very own evening, and unforgettable.

We came into the house to find a tear-stained mother holding a sobbing toddler in her arms. Norma had red, swollen eyes and a huge professional bandage on her right middle finger.

"My dear, what's wrong?" asked my father, kneeling on the rug in his anguish, all primroses forgotten. "What's happened?"

Mamma burst into tears, but managed to explain that the children had been playing in the garden at the back whilst the neighbours were mowing their lawn. Norma, who was only four, had got through the strand-wire fence to watch, and the neighbour had playfully run the mower towards her. Half laughing and half afraid Norma had tried to stop it with her hands, and had lost the top of her finger. Mamma had sensibly wrapped her hand in a clean towel, put her in the push-chair and rushed her to the doctor. They had just got back, and Mamma could do nothing but cuddle the hurt, frightened little girl. Our return was a great relief to them.

Daddy first made a cup of tea, and then some cocoa for Norma, who in spite of her pain was very ready for sleep. Whilst they got her to bed I wandered out into the garden where Peter and Doreen were still playing, and was puzzled by their apparent lack of concern. That such deep happiness could, without warning, be cut through by tragedy was food for thought. The evening had been memorable in more ways than one.

CHAPTER NINE

Lucy and I went to school by turning right from our road and going past some scruffy allotments behind a hawthorn hedge, across the small railway bridge and past the National School. This is now St. Nicholas Junior School, still doing yeoman service despite its ancient bricks and mortar. We then turned left at the corner into Pound Street, passing the Rectory, an enormous, dreary pile on the right, and at the end of this street we had only to cross the road at Kimber's Corner and enter by the big school gates. At the gates of course, avidly licking her pencil, was a monitress, waiting to note down the names of 'stragglers', (nearly late), and real dyed-in-the-wool latecomers.

We set off together from the house, but were soon separated by our respective groups of friends. Lily, Vera and Muriel and I went a little ahead and forgot entirely about Lucy and her friends following up. Just as we were crossing to enter the big school gates what should we see but Lucy and Laura and Janie approaching from the other railway bridge, past Dean's, our grocer's. My jaw dropped. The three were grinning with horrid superiority as they arrived, neck and neck with us.

"Where've you been?"

"We know a new way to school. We didn't come your way."

"Which way did you go?"

"Ah, we're not telling you! We're keeping it a secret."

"Yes, we don't want all the little kids following us." Laura was always a reliable back-up for Lucy.

"Don't call us kids. Mamma doesn't like it."

" 'Mamma doesn't like it'. Oh dear, what a shame!"

'Kids' was another swear word that Lucy and I had picked up at school, but were not allowed to use. Our latest was 'shut-up', which I was loth to relinquish. It was such a full-bodied, effective word to use.

"Tell us, Lucy, go on."

"No. We're only going to let our friends go that way. We found it first."

"If it's a road everyone can go on it."

"Ah, but you see, it's private, and no little ones can go on it."

I felt sure of being able to get the information out of Lucy after we had gone to bed. Away from the schoolchildren we were more evenly matched, and in any case Lucy really was the gentle and affectionate child everyone kept telling me she was. I could usually get round her. But during dinner time at home I had a better, and more immediate idea. When Lucy and Laura set off for school again I encouraged my gang to lag behind picking buttercups. When Lucy and Laura had turned right I waited and watched, and to my amazement saw them disappear through a small gap in the hawthorn hedge, and go running through the allotments. Beckoning on my followers I also went through the gap and pranced along behind. We were soon spotted, and the bigger children ran on, with me, Lily, Vera and Muriel in hot pursuit. We all emerged quite soon in Bartholomew Street, and had only to cross the bridge by Station Road to arrive at the gates. We had broken their secret.

The hedge gap was soon made into a wide opening, the scruffy cabbages and run-up sprouts lay down and died under piles of sand and gravel. The new road was growing, and was henceforth in general use by the public. To us it remained the 'New Road' for years, even when the neat rows of houses were occupied, and dignified by the name of 'St. Michael's Road'.

Thus we no longer needed to go past the National School, which was so much older than ours was. This was a relief, as there were frequent quarrels and sometimes a fight, between their pupils and ours. A sort of inverted snobbery made them resent us passing by from our new houses to our fairly new school. They assumed we thought ourselves better than they, so we came to believe that we were. Tradition had it that the dirty children went to the National School, although I can recall some very dirty specimens, (detectable by the olfactory method), present in the Council School. Vera and I, and Lucy and Laura had some most invigorating quarrels standing on the pavement opposite St. Nicholas School, and learnt some intriguing facts.

"Your silly old school doesn't win scholarships." Laura shouted in passing.

"Oh, yes we do then. You can ask Governess." Susie shouted back.

"Governess! What's Governess?" I asked derisively.

"She's our head teacher, and she's ever so strict. Stricter than your Governess."

"We don't have a Governess. It's a silly old name. We call her the Headmistress."

"Oh, the headmistress." Susie minced and prinked and pursed her lips.

"Posh, aren't you? You lot think you're everybody."

"She's just as strict as your stupid old Governess. She's got a cane."

"Well, our Governess has got a cane and a strap, and she keeps you in, too sometimes."

"That's because you're naughtier than us. All the rough kids go to your school." 'Kids'. Lucy had actually sworn!

This squabble went on and on, but luckily it remained verbal. The protagonist, Susie, was a pleasant little girl, with whom we later made friends.

On Saturdays Lucy and I, with Peter and Norma, and later with Doreen too, traversed the same route to spend our Saturday pennies. This was a family ritual. As soon as dinner was over Daddy, for whom Saturday afternoon was a half day off, would produce his purse and slowly, with exaggerated ceremony, would give us each a penny. The pennies would be cradled, and looked at, and compared for dates and for pictures of the sovereign. Discussion then arose on all sides as to which shop was nearer, and which better, and which gave best value for money. These were the days of cheap, imaginative confectionary by Barrett's, licquorice daddy-long-leg's, raspberry pips, golden toffee bars, coconut chips, sweet potatoes, sweet peas, gob-stoppers. The choice was very difficult.

We usually went to Miss Empson's shop, next to our school. This little shop must have done very well in its position next to a large school. It was a double fronted shop, (now a dress shop), with one window for sweets and one for groceries and as each side had a separate counter Miss Empson spent her life going from one side of the shop to the other. There were two steps from the street going down into it, and a bell clanged as the door was opened. During the rush hour just before school this shop became very crowded, but I never witnessed any shop-lifting. Perhaps Miss Empson's rather fierce expression was conducive to honesty, although I learned later that this was due to her short sight and very thick glasses. She was, in fact, the mildest of persons, kindly and almost timid. In the dark unknown living quarters behind the shop she cared for an invalid father, who, although never seen, gave us a feeling that Miss Empson was backed by a strong, male authority.

Baby Doreen had her cot in our bedroom, and was always asleep when Lucy and I went up to bed. The last injunction we received at bedtime was always,

"No noise, mind. I don't want Doreen woken up."

On Summer evenings, when the outside world was wide awake with sounds of children, wirelesses, and lawnmowers, and the sweet smell of freshly cut grass floated over our double bed it was difficult to go to sleep. We talked quietly, listening to Doreen's gentle breathing.

"I'm getting a book. It's too light to go to sleep."

Lucy got out and padded across to the shelf, holding her calico nightie off the floor very daintily with one hand. She bounced back into bed and laid the book on the counterpane, then went into her thorough tucking-in routine, without which she never felt secure. The book slid off the bed onto the lino with a bang. I gave an exaggerated theatrical sigh.

"Lucy, honestly!"

"Well, you said you couldn't sleep, so why not be properly awake? Do you want to read the book?"

Lucy sometimes displayed an icy logic which was unanswerable. I picked up the book. It was Amy le Feuvre's 'Amy's Secret', which we had both read several times.

There was to be no reading that night though, for at that moment Doreen turned over and opened a bright eye. No doubt the bang had wakened her. Seeing us both in bed she probably thought it was morning and scrambled up at the side of the cot.

"Lie down, Doreen. Go to sleep."

Not she! She rattled the cot bars and broke into a happy babble, intersperesed with snatches of song.

Lucy looked at me meaningfully.

"Now look what you've done. You've woken her up."

"It wasn't me. You dropped the book. Mamma will be cross. Doreen, sh . . ."

"Sh", said Doreen, smiling broadly, and rattling the bars with all her sleep-gathered energy.

"Shut up," said Lucy.

"Shut up," said I.

Doreen loved this game. "Shubbup," she shouted.

We were delighted by her clever naughtiness, and the more we laughed the more she shouted.

"Shubbup. Shubbup."

Mamma came in, of course.

"Whatever's going on in here?"

Doreen turned to her with an angelic smile and said,

"Shubbup."

Lucy and I slithered down under the covers and blushed into our calico.

"Now I wonder where she's learnt that," Mamma said to no-one in particular. She laid the little girl down in the cot and tucked her in.

"No more talking, you two. It's time you all went to sleep."

We lay there quaking with silent laughter, because from the cot we heard one final, happy, pianissimo, "Shubbup."

I always enjoyed shopping with my mother. I liked the streets, and the insides and outsides of shops. Often there were four of us, two little ones in the pram and two bigger ones holding on to the metal framework. Our groceries came from the International Stores, a big shop in Bartholomew Street. They had a strong rival in the shop next door, smaller in itself but very well-supported, the Home and Colonial Stores. Vera's father was the manager of the Home and Colonial Stores, so tact was needed when discussing shopping matters. Another friend's father was the manager of our grocer's. The International Stores was a spacious shop with a frontage made more attractive by the long strings of round red and yellow cheeses which were a part of my hymnology. Inside were two long counters, very high, with several tall chairs for the comfort of weary customers. There were no very long waits, however, as there were plenty of courteous and willing assistants. At the cash desk a large, pleasant lady sat all day receiving payments and dispatching change by means of an overhead cable railway.

Mamma shopped carefully. There was never money to spare.

"Half of your Sylvan Glen butter, please, and a half of your own marg."

Out came the butter pats and a piece of greaseproof paper. Cut, slap, dab, press the sides, the ends, onto the scales; another shaving from the main supply, another slap, dab and press, and the neat rectangle was set aside.

"Ninepence halfpenny, Madam. And the next?"

"Tea, please. A quarter of Lyons' Green Label."

"Eightpence."

"A packet of 'Red, white and blue' coffee, please. A small one."

"You know there's chicory in it, Madam?"

"Yes, that's all right. How much?"

"Eleven and a half."

"Thank you. And some cheese. What do you recommend?"

"If you want a nice strong cheese, Madam, you want our English Cheddar. Very strong. Try it."

The assistant produced a little metal tube like an apple corer and poked it into the huge cheese to get out a 'taster'. My mother ate it, slowly and thoughtfully.

"Mm . . ." she said, before swallowing it, "That'll do. Half a pound please, or a little less."

"Seven and a half, Madam, that nice piece." He put it aside with the other things, and rested his hands on their finger tips to await further requirements.

"Sugar, please. Two pounds of gran."

Hands slid along a lower shelf behind the counter and produced a bright blue bag. There was a huge tub of white sugar at the back, with a scoop, from which he filled the bag with uncanny accuracy, needing no more than a second on the scale to check it. With deft fingers he folded in the top edges, and put it aside.

"Nine, the sugar."

The collection on the counter grew and grew. Self-raising flour, currants, sultanas, Foster Clark's soup square, a bar of Sunlight soap, a packet of dried eggs, Bournville cocoa, International Orange marmalade, International plum jam, all of it was packed into two big old bags and stowed in the capacious well of the pram. Notes were pressed onto the little overhead railcar, the cord was pulled, and we waited. When the change arrived Mamma sorted it into her housekeeping purse and away we went.

"I don't know," she murmured, as she skilfully manoeuvered the pram with its two occupants, its two hangers-on, and its load of shopping down from the kerb to cross the street, "I don't know. If prices go much higher I don't know how we're going to live."

We had crossed the road to go to Leach's, the butcher, where yet another friend's father worked. I detested the butcher's shop, its smell, its bloody appearance, and the devastating sound of its terrible bright choppers. I preferred to wait outside and look after our pram.

"I must just pop into McIlroy's, then we'll go home." Mamma told us sympathetically. The little ones were bored by that time, and probably hungry.

McIlroy's was the draper shop next to the Post Office, now a furniture shop. It seemed to me a big and interesting place, supplying a useful line in haberdashery which is now difficult to find in Newbury. It is irritating to have to buy buttons in fives and tens if you only want two, elastic in packets with unwanted yardage, fancy pins in fancy boxes when all you need is a paper of them. Mamma's needs were simple this time, two and a half yards of knicker elastic, measured on the counter's edge, a reel of number forty cotton and a skein of grey mending, for which she paid a total of one and three.

We walked towards home, calling in at Robert's, the baker's, now in the hands of another 'Baker', an electrical dealer. This was, to a small child, a 'high' shop, approached by several steps. Mamma bought a small brown loaf for fourpence-halfpenny, and chatted awhile to Mrs. Roberts, whilst I gazed at the wonderful assortment of halfpenny cakes in the window. It was a sunny day, and the flies, attracted by the heated glass and the smell of sugar, were congregated thickly on all the little cakes. My interest however was gastronomic, not entomological.

"Can we have a cake today, Mamma? We haven't had a fancy cake for ages."

"Not today, Jane. If you could see what I've got left in my purse to last the rest of the week you wouldn't ask."

Whilst my mother unloaded the shopping and got our tea ready I wandered out into the sunshine alone. I was wearing a recently demoted 'best' dress of natural tussore silk with a double flounced skirt finished with bright green scallops. Lucy and I both had one. I absent-mindedly climbed onto one of the little concrete posts which were set in pairs to mark each small entrance path, and gazed about me, doing no harm at all, just meditating. A sharp voice behind me said,

"You think you're everybody, don't you, standing up there in that silly old dress!"

It was Doris, an off-and-on friend of ours. I jumped down almost guiltily.

"I suppose it's your best?"

"Yes. Well, no. It was my best, but now it's my second best."

"I know. I've seen it. If I had it I'd have it for my very, very oldest, so there."

I was too young for repartee. It was an art I learnt later, so I had no reply. But I had a vivid picture of Mamma sitting for hours and hours putting the double rows of scallops on our two frocks, and my eyes filled at Doris's belittlement. I rushed indoors, blinded with tears, to find Mamma unscathed by criticism, slicing the bread for tea. I poured out my unhappiness, but could not explain the true reason for it.

"You don't need to cry like that. Don't let other children upset you so. I'm surprised, I must say, to find Doris being so spiteful."

She stood with one hand in her apron pocket and the other on her hip, somewhat at a loss to understand my excess of grief.

"Now listen," she said, "and I'll tell you something. When you've got something nice and someone says nasty things about it, it means they're jealous. They wish they had one the same, but they haven't, so if you're a nice little girl you should feel sorry for them."

I was not yet in such a state of grace that I could feel sorry for Doris, but even so this point of view was a great comfort to me. I dried my tears.

"Look, Doreen's waiting for her tea. You go and give her her crust."

This was a happy task. All our babies used to cut their teeth on the crusty edges of loaves, as no money was ever spent on rusks. All our loaves, therefore, had long corners sliced off all round, which made each slice a funny shape. We thought this was the right way for bread and butter to be. Doreen eagerly accepted the crust, and the sunny smile she gave me put an end to my grief.

Our bread was always spread with what we spoke of as 'the butter', but which was really a half-and-half mixture. Each shopping day when the margarine and butter were brought home our mother would mix it together into one mass in a basin, under a system called 'making the butter go round the week'. In cold weather it was left in front of the fire before mixing, to soften a little, but in this hot weather it was nearly always at melting point. There was no cool place anywhere for it. I used to like watching Mamma channel it to and fro with the knife blade.

"Mamma, that's adultery, what you're doing!"

She stopped in mid-stroke. I could almost see the shock waves pulsing out between her parted lips.

"What do you mean?"

"Well, you're mixing something good with something bad."

She drew a deep, hissing breath, as one gathering strength.

"To start with, Jane, margarine is not something bad. I'm mixing two good things together. And to go on with, if I did mix something bad with the butter that would be, not adultery, but adulteration."

(Oh dear, oh dear!)

"And I think it's time you stopped saying that word altogether. You've kept on about it for days. I don't want to hear it any more. It's not a very nice word."

"But the man in chapel read a story about it, to all the people. He didn't think it was a bad word. It's in the Bible."

"Yes, I know, but you remember what I say. There are some things in the Bible that we don't talk about."

This I had already discovered. My Bible opened itself at the page where Jacob and Esau struggled together in the womb. I had recently set out on the long, fighting journey towards sexual understanding.

When we began to have difficulty in seeing out from under our fringes Daddy used to cut our hair. He had of course, a special pair of scissors which he sharpened himself and put away in a particular place each time. The client had to stand up on a stool and keep still whilst he went round, skrrr, skrrr, scraping with the comb to ensure a level and even finish, a perfectionist in this as in all things. When he had done he shook off the towel, blew all round the neck to banish stray hairs and called for the next customer. On one of my appointments I had my ear cut, not badly of course, but it bled alarmingly. After this incident he allowed me to place a finger on each ear lobe whenever I ascended the stool, to make certain I grew up with the usual two.

He also eased the drain on the family purse by repairing all our shoes. This was a Saturday afternoon job, as he was at work on Saturday mornings. First the leather had to be purchased, and I often went with him to choose a piece. There were several shoe-repairing shops in Newbury when I was little, Walker's in Cheap Street, Noakes's in Oxford Street, Rivers's in Bartholomew Street. Whilst Daddy was going carefully through the pieces of leather, trying to compute the various factors of size, thickness, quality, evenness of weight and price, I was just the right height to sniff them all and fill my lungs with their satisfying, living smell. Daddy, of course, had brought a cut-out paper pattern of the exact size and shape of the soles and heels to be mended, and was engaged in a newspaper jig-saw on his probable choice.

I wandered round, reading the advertisements for Phillips' 'Stick-a-Soles for your dainty shoes', and Blakey's Protectors 'for all the family'. I particularly liked the little dog walking in the rain with four wellington boots.

The actual work was done sitting down on a doormat on the floor. Daddy had short, sharp knives to cut out the shapes, nails, hammers, and a cobbler's 'foot'. When the soles and heels were affixed he tapped in a generous edging of Blakey's, and ran the heel ball around the cut leather. These sturdy repairs lasted many months.

CHAPTER TEN

When we were a little older Lucy and I began to go further afield, especially in the school holidays. We played a lot at Laura's house. She had a sister of my age called Jeanie, and we got on well as a group of four. Sometimes when our mother thought we were playing in their garden we would all go off into the town, especially if it was a market day.

Newbury has a good Market Place, and the Thursday and Saturday markets have always attracted people from all the surrounding villages as well as the town population. Today's markets are as big as ever, and as well supported, but they have changed in character. All the stalls now seem to have the stability and reputation of shops. They and their owners are there every week, as familiar to the shoppers as Woolworth's and Marks and Spencer's, but the charlatans have gone. Before the Second World War there were always men who seemed merely to occupy a patch of ground, with no stall or cover of any kind. Using just a little table or bench they would collect a small crowd by shouting, or by using a rattle or hooter, and demonstrate their lines there and then. They sold hem-stitchers, stain-removers, magic soap, incredible polishes, and infallible pills to the gullible, of whom there were plenty. There was no Trade Descriptions Act in force then. We enjoyed standing around to watch and listen.

There were fruit-vendors who stood on boxes surrounded by their wares, and selling them very successfully by a high-pressure technique.

"Look at this! Look at this! Bananas here. A yard long and a foot wide. Come on, there must be a couple of dozen or more there. One and six. I'm givin' 'em away. Who's going to have them for one and six? Now look 'ere. I'm putting not one, not two, but three oranges on top of that lot. You've never seen a bargain like it. You'll never see another one like it. Never in your life. And again, lady over there. The only one with any brains. I congratulate you my love. And now, look at this!"

His voice, already hoarse, rose to squeak of incredibility.

"You've never seen lettuces like this anywhere, I'll bet you a pound. Who's going to take me on? No, I knew you wouldn't. Look, lettuce, lettuce, let us rejoice! And a tomato to go with it. Threepence. I'm giving it away. It cost me more than that to get it here. Lady over there. And another."

When I was quite young there were high rows of chicken-coops in Newbury market. With one row standing on another they made a row wall about four feet high and twelve coops long, in which were hens for sale, and sometimes, in Spring, fluffy yellow chickens. For me the hen-coops were an attractive feature of the market, noisy, full of life and just on a child's eye-level. On Saturdays we often went shopping in the market with our parents, and came home with the well of the pram filled with bananas, farthing oranges and crisp, English apples. Half a banana with bread and butter was a frequent breakfast menu.

On cattle market days, of course, the little street was far from quiet. Loads of cattle, pigs and sheep were trucked in, protesting loudly and driven with threats to their pens. More entertaining for us it was to see them walked into market by farm workers with sticks and hoarse voices. Our natural interest in animals and commerce were greatly enhanced by the thrill of danger. There was always the risk of our being chased round the pens by a cow, or even of being tossed and gored by a bull. But the greatest threat of all, and the one sometimes realised, was of being driven off by 'the man', using the same tones with which he addressed the animals. Those were authoritarian days.

Some of the animals we enjoyed watching were due to embark on their last, short journey, but of this we knew nothing. I was however to find out, and before very long.

I had a school friend called Connie, whose father worked at the abattoir. Connie and I arranged to go to the swimming baths one summer afternoon, so I called for her at her house.

"I haven't got any change, Connie," her mother told her. "Call in and ask your dad for a penny."

"Ooh, yes, and he'll give us a penny for some sweets too." Connie informed me. I was all in favour.

We walked through Bartholomew Street, passed the Parish Church and turned into Northcroft Lane. Here we could see the water slipping quietly under the shapely, centuries-old bridge, and some very old, low-lying buildings right by the water's edge.

"Here's where my dad works." Connie lifted the latch and went in. I followed. Then I stood appalled at what I saw. Connie's gentle dad was there, smiling at us, wearing a long, white stained jacket, and holding a lamb by its two front feet. He gathered the back legs in his large hands as well, and calmly slit its throat. Then he threw it, still jerking and trembling onto a long shelf with other carcases, and gave his attention to his little daughter. Connie was prattling on about no change in Mummy's purse, and prettily suggesting that a penny each for sweets would not come amiss. I stood shocked into pale-faced silence, watching the blood of the lamb run red down the runnel.

Connie's dad rubbed his hands dry on the long, white smock and thrust one into a pocket to find some pennies. Soon we were on the way to the sweet shop, spyrogyra and happiness, but I was haunted by the penny in my hand. It seemed like blood money.

Almost opposite this long-demolished abattoir, in Northcroft Lane, are two buildings which have had a long and influential history in the town. The Salvation Army Citadel has been there as long as I can remember, unchanged and flourishing. Almost next door is the Temperance Hall, which started as a workshop, became a school, then later a warehouse. In 1875 it was taken over and re-modelled by the Temperance Society, and used as a meeting house for the upholders of teetotalism. Lucy and I enrolled very early as Junior members in a club called 'The Little White Ribboners'. We were invited twice a year to their tea-party and meeting, and were asked to wear a little white ribbon bow pinned to our dress or jumper.

We looked forward to these bun-fights. There was a good tea, with cakes and tarts and lemonade, and then we played organised games, 'Oranges and Lemons', and 'Nuts in May' to help the tea go down. Lucy and I were pleased to see Susie from the National School there.

After the games came the nub of the thing.

"Now, all sit down on a chair, children, and be very quiet, because Mr. . . . is going to tell us a story."

Everyone did as they asked us to. Not even the fairly big boys showed any behaviour problem.

The story followed the usual moral, sentimental, Victorian pattern. A slum family, reduced to poverty and debt by the father's spending his Friday wage on strong drink was redeemed to respectability and a cottage in the country when Father accidentally came within the sphere of the Temperance Society (via his little daughter). It was a moving tale, and our appreciation of its moral was not left to chance.

The Temperance Hall in Northcroft Lane is now serving Newbury as the Arts workshop. The clause in the deeds forbidding the sale of alcohol on the premises still obtains, and is observed, but an imaginative reading of the word 'sale' allows the clause to be circumvented.

The care of five young children is a strain on even the healthiest woman, and our mother was not in good health. Washing day, in the pre-machine age, was particularly hard for her, with two toddlers at home all the time and seven people to wash for. So it came about that my father arranged some help for her. On washing days (Mondays, of course) a lady called Mrs. Coles arrived just as we were setting out for school, to help with the heavy task.

The procedure was as follows.

First of all the copper, which was used as a working surface all the week, had to be cleared of such things as the peg-bag, the string-tin, old bottles, Vim on a saucer, packets of assorted screws and nails. Then the copper had to be filled, bucket by bucket with soft water from the soft-water tap in the coalshed. The fire-hole had to be cleared of last week's ash and any additional rubbish which had been poked in since. A proper fire was then laid with sticks on newspaper, and at last came the moment to light it with a match. When the sticks began to crackle coal was added, brought in on a shovel from the coalshed. As this caught and reddened the water began to feel tepid when the great lid was lifted for testing with the hand.

The time which it took to become usefully hot was spent by Mrs. Coles and Mamma in sorting, whites in one pile and coloureds in another, socks and dusters in another. The coloured garments needed thought, as very few of the dyes were fast, and one red dress carelessly thrown in could mean pink patches on everything else. The whites could then be put to soak in the two-handled galvanised bath, with a handful of soda crystals.

"Mrs. Coles uses too much soda," I heard Mamma say quite often to Daddy, when all our brown woollen socks had turned out streaky. "I keep telling her, but she goes on doing just the same."

One other job had to be done before the actual elbow-wetting ritual could begin. Mrs. Coles would get down the long, unsectioned bar of Sunlight soap, which had been hardening a week or two on the shelf, and cut it into pieces. Her huge, red hands, with their seventeen stone back-up drove the knife through the rock-like soap with Herculean ease. The resulting sections had hard cutting edges almost like glass, and I liked to handle them, knowing that a short time in the hot soda water would smooth the edges to curves. Normally I was at school while all this happened, but there were the holidays.

Everything was now prepared. Mrs. Coles got the clanking bucket and scraped it along the stone floor beneath the copper tap, took down the key and turned on. Boiling, scummy water hissed into the bucket, with steam enough for a Turkish bath. Mrs. Coles heaved it up and poured it into this two-handled bath where the whites were soaking. In went her bare red hands and arms, and she began to soap and rub each garment, getting redder about the face and neck with every one. Mamma drew off some more boiling water to wash the coloured things in a separate tub, put coal on the fire and soap in the copper. As Mrs. Coles washed each white object she lifted the copper lid and dropped it in to boil. You could not see across the scullery for steam.

Since the hot water in the copper was now soapy for the boil all rinsing was done in cold. This was no hardship in mild weather, but must have been a painful business in the depths of winter.

Our washing line stretched the whole length of the garden and was always filled on Mondays, with a few odds and ends left over to be dried over the gas stove. A wet washing day was gruesome! We had no wringer or mangle, and all the dripping clothes hung around indoors, garment over garment, becoming impregnated with cooking smells.

This was about the stage reached when we used to arrive from school for our dinner. It was a depressing reception. Dinner consisted of bread and cheese, with perhaps an apple, and was partaken of by Mrs. Coles as well, who sat at the table and effectively blocked out the light. She never spoke a word, but stared at us all with her round blue eyes as if she had never seen a child before. In her presence we too were silent, although Lucy and I were hard put to it sometimes to check our giggling.

This simple repast over we scampered off, with considerable relief, to school. Mrs. Coles then cleared up the scullery, washed the floor with soapy water from the copper, which she then emptied and dried. These chores completed she put on her funny flat hat and pinned it alarmingly, gratefully accepted half-a-crown and went on her silent way to a home I could never visualise.

This copper was something of a tyrant in our house. Since the bathroom was given over to photography the copper was our only source of hot water, other than by the kettleful. So bath night became a family affair. We all had to bath when the copper was on. As little ones we were bathed in the same two-handled tub in which Mrs. Coles soaked the whites, and very pleasant it was, positioned in front of the copper fire with the little door open. Whatever one was engrossed in the bath had to be taken immediately the copper boiled in order that more water could be put in to keep the supply going. Our copper would brook no delay of attention. If the person summoned to the bath did not get on with it there would be a hiss, a fizz, a house full of steam and a flood on the stone floor of the kitchen. Mopping it up was a horrible job. As we grew older we had to carry up our own bucket of boiling water, and it is terrifying to think of the risks involved. The bucket had to be carried through the scullery, through the living-room, up the stairs and into the bathroom, lifted up and emptied into the bath. We never had an accident. My father, so gifted in many ways, never solved this organisational problem. It was not until we were grown up, with earnings of our own, that we sorted it out.

CHAPTER ELEVEN

"I wish we had a pack of cards, don't you?"

It was the summer holidays, and Lucy and I had spent a wet afternoon in our shed with Laura and Jeanie, playing 'Beggar your Neighbour', 'Rummy' and 'Spoof'. We had rigged up a table using the sawing horse, and further supports of blocks of wood, with our little blackboard laid across them. To us, unused to playing cards, these games were exhilarating and almost magical, but the afternoon ended, Laura and Jeanie went home with their pack of cards, leaving us sheltering from the heavy rain in the shed, which seemed suddenly gloomy and unfriendly.

"Do you think Mamma and Daddy have got some on the top shelf?" The top shelf of the dresser was inaccessible to us still; we could not even reach it by standing on a chair.

"Shouldn't think so. Let's go and ask her."

Lucy's requests were a little more likely to meet with a favourable reply than mine. Lucy was not a nuisance.

Mamma was bustling from room to room, getting tea ready.

"Cards? You mean playing cards?"

"Those with Jacks and aces and numbers and hearts, and all that."

"Not 'all that', Lucy. Say what you mean."

"Well, a proper set of cards, like Laura's got."

"No, we haven't got any like that. Only happy families."

"Why not?" That was me, being a persistent nuisance.

"Our parents didn't play cards, and wouldn't have them in the house."

"Why not?"

"Oh, I don't know. They thought it not quite right. I don't see any harm in a game of cards myself, but we've never had any."

And that was that. We were to be dependent for ever on Laura's and Jeanie's pack, and they were going on holiday the next day. Lucy and I were Spoof-crazy, and could envisage a long succession of Spoofless days ahead. We lay in bed that evening whispering quietly about our deprivation.

"Why don't we make some?" Lucy suggested. "We could cut some out and crayon them. It won't matter if the picture's a bit funny as long as we know which card it's supposed to be."

I was enthusiastic at first, then

"It'll take us ages to do fifty-two of them."

"Only twenty-six each. We could do them in a day."

"What shall we make them with? We'll need heaps of cardboard."

"We've got our shoe boxes," Lucy reminded me, "and perhaps Peter will give us his if we let him play after."

"We'll have to cut them very small even then, and it's hard to write tiny little numbers with thick crayons."

"Well, we'll have to write the numbers with a pencil, and colour them a bit. If we start after breakfast we could get them finished by the afternoon."

There came a warning snuffle from the cot, and Doreen turned over in her sleep, so we fell silent, in happy anticipation of a rewarding day to follow.

Peter was easily persuaded to part with his shoe box, so that made three. We were up against an immediate problem. The cardboard was too thick to yield to the small pair of scissors, and we had only one large pair, so we took turns at the painful job of cutting strips and little oblongs. Despair gripped us again when we found that even with three boxes we had not enough card.

"They'll all have to be cut in half."

"Never mind. They'll be dinky little playing cards."

We cut, and numbered, and coloured all day long, and by early evening the pack of cards was complete. Perhaps 'pack' was not the perfect collective term, because that was what they would not do. Fashioned from stout, old-type shoe boxes, our fifty-two cards made a wobbly stack eleven inches high, which could not be persuaded to stay stacked. New methods of play had to be adopted, and new rules formulated. For instance, since the small, thick cards could not be held fan-wise as a hand, we had to spread them out on the table surface, face up, which left our playing strengths exposed. This we overcame by getting three big books each and standing them up to form booths, in the privacy of which we manoeuvred to win. Since 'Spoof' requires a large space for laying out the cards in suits the whole table was covered with our game. Peter was too young to play, but he was very interested, and liked to kneel up on a chair to watch our mysterious rituals with bits of his shoe box.

Since we had only the one table it seemed that whenever we got to a crisis in the game, and had our tongues poking out with excitement, there came a dreaded call,

"Clear the table, please."

and we pushed all the cards into two paper bags, leaving the issue for ever undecided.

It rained so continuously for a few days that the drains became choked and the gulleys could cope with no more. Water poured down the road, and rose up the sides of the little posts. We all gathered at the window to look out at our flood, and still the rain hissed down. Our neighbour went out in gum-boots and mack, and poked the gulley with a long stick, but to our impish delight it was no remedy. He went back indoors, wet and sheepish, conscious of a row of eyes at every window. We speculated in excited voices as to the possible depth of the flood, and the likelihood of our being cut off from the rest of England. It was all of two inches deep.

Suddenly the rain stopped and the sun came out. Everything began gleaming and steaming, the children put on wellingtons and went out to paddle on the road. With disappointing rapidity the flood subsided, and half-an-hour later we were once again in touch with the world.

In fine weather the large central green was always alive with children. It was a wonderful place for us all to meet and play in safety, within sight of our homes. The green became invisibly divided by custom into a football area, where the big boys played endless games of soccer, the little kids' bit, at the extreme opposite corner, and a large middle area for middle-aged children. Inevitably a path of bare earth appeared crossing the green from end to end, and to counter this the local council erected bars at either end to prevent people from using it as a short cut instead of going round by the footpath. These bars were smooth, metal poles, set about three feet above the ground in solid concrete posts, ideal for swinging, somersaulting, and an endless variety of gymnastic activities. The 'bars' at both ends became favourite playing places, and induced fierce competition for the invention of bolder and wilder acrobatics.

One very hot day in late May we were all playing on the green. It was the Whitsun holiday, with perfect weather, and we sat in the long grass making butter-cup chains, at the little kids' end, of course. We could even hide, by lying down, so long was the field growth. I was hiding, on my own, and quite happy, although the others had forgotten about finding me. Buttercups, varnished by the hot sun, daisies, not so tall but flushed with heat, feathery grasses designed for feeling, sturdy red-leaved sorrel sour as vinegar, clovers, white and spicy, pink and three-leaved, birds' eyes and the flat circle of dull plantain leaves. What else? I inched forward on my stomach. A lady-bird. Come on, little lady-bird. I'm not going to squash you. I only want to count your coloured spots. Didn't get the chance. It showed its other wings before it flew off, like teacher told us about. I wonder what teacher's doing today. Having a cup of tea, I expect. I want a drink. It's so hot!

I left my private world of long grass and ran indoors.

"Mamma, I'm going to have a drink of water. It's too hot."

"Too hot! How do you think I feel in here all the time with the oven on? I'd give anything to go outside and play."

I felt guilty and said no more, but I lifted the enamel mug from its hook and helped myself to a long, cool drink from the tap. I replaced the mug, unwashed, on its hook and went off out into the sun again.

During my few minutes indoors a horse and cart had arrived, and was right up on the green, where traffic, obviously, was not allowed. The horse was already busy renewing its strength, and two men had got out of the cart each carrying a scythe. They proceeded to mow the grass, working their way systematically from edge to edge of the green, leaving the lovely, long grasses and all the flowers in wilting swathes. We stood watching in a crooked, curious line, and whenever the deadly instruments moved up a row we all jumped back, shrieking. If any bold spirit dared for a moment to show off by holding his ground the man in charge shouted,

"Get back, you kids, or I'll 'ave yer feet off!"

It took them two days to hand mow the whole green. They knocked off at five the first day, leaving half of our lovely field shorn, and strewn with long green cuttings, whilst the big boys' end was still long and tangly. I walked sadly around, kicking the limp grass and the faded flowers, remembering the richness of its morning state.

"I wish they didn't cut it, don't you?"

Vera was not sure.

"It won't make our feet wet when it rains."

"Well, we can always play in the road when it rains. I wonder who told them they could cut it."

"It's the men from the Council, my mum told me. They get paid for it, you know, like work."

Vera was stooping down and gathering a heap of grass cuttings in her hands. I helped her, and soon we had a high pile.

"Sit on it." Vera said.

I jumped as high as possible and landed on the pile, which yielded gently with a rebound. We rebuilt it, and Vera had a turn. Other children copied us, and soon the little kids' area was full of shouting and laughter.

"I know. Let's make a house," I suggested.

We gathered huge piles of grass cuttings and laid them out in lines to represent walls, with gaps for doors. We made many rooms, a huge house, and then played families in it, treating our walls with great realism and entering only by the doors.

One of our favourite games, needing a wide space and many children was 'Eggo Remove'. It may have been 'Egg of Remove', or even 'Eggory Move'. We never saw it spelt. It is played with a ball, thrown back over the head by the starter, who simultaneously shouts a name. The named person chases the ball whilst everyone else runs as hard as possible away from it. The chaser, having picked up the ball, holds it high, calling 'Eggo Remove', at which signal every player stands stock still. Holding the ball, the chaser is allowed to take three strides towards the nearest player, and tries to hit his feet by throwing the ball. If he succeeds that player re-starts the game by throwing the ball back over his head. If not, all the others run away again, and the chaser has to recapture the ball and repeat the routine.

It was a very popular game, made even faster and more exciting by the newly-mown grass. I regretted the rape of so much richness, but soon observed that, in common with primroses, blackberries and Christmas, it enjoyed an annual re-birth, as well as an annual death.

A little later in that same summer another horse-drawn cart arrived, providing a new delight. A local farmer, a Mr. Cory, had filled his cart with bushels of surplus apples. It was an 'apple year', and there was no market for the 'seconds'. Mr. Cory led his horse slowly along the road around the green, and threw out apples all over the grass. A few children scrambled for them, screaming, and attracted others. Magically, within minutes, the green was covered with running, shouting children all picking up apples as fast as they could. Some took time out to fetch a paper bag, but in doing so wasted valuable apple-collecting time. I was filling my brief skirt with them, and by the time Mr. Cory's cart was empty the skirt was perilously heavy. I walked home carefully, controlling a risky front wobble, and there on the doorstep was Daddy, busy photographing the lively scene.

CHAPTER TWELVE

To me the dullest time of the whole year was the post-Christmas period. The festivities over and summer so far ahead, I imagined that life was going to be very boring for a very long time. This year however, would be different. No sooner had we started back to school than we were told by our teachers to work extra hard as there was to be an exhibition. I did not know what that was, but remembered the word to ask at home.

The subsequent weeks revealed all. The exhibition was to be held, in the Corn Exchange, (to me, the Cornix Change), and good work from each class in each school would be on view to parents, and to the public. I wondered what the inside of the Corn Exchange looked like. Will all the good work be pinned up round the walls, like it is in our class? Will they take our sum books and our composition books? If they do shall we get new ones? I hope we can do it with pencil, or else they won't choose mine.

The days went by and class distinctions arose. Some were chosen, some were not. All of us were excited. We did have to write with ink, but I was mastering that inimical nib, so my story was chosen, mounted on black paper and laid aside with others. It was called 'A Day in the Life of a Donkey', a title chosen by our teacher. I also exhibited a poem written at home called 'Fire Fairies', and a sheet of sums which the teacher called 'miscellaneous examples'. I still had no idea what an exhibition looked like.

When the great day came I went with Daddy to the Corn Exchange. It was uncomfortably crowded with grown-up people, and quite different from what I had expected. Large boards had been set up for the display of written work at all stages, all well-mounted and attractively arranged. My story was there, and my poem, and on another board my squared sheet of miscellaneous examples. There were paintings, pencil sketches, designs and drawings, and meticulously copied pages in joined-up writing by the older children, whose cleverness seemed beyond belief. But the section which held me spellbound was the craftwork, embroidered handkerchiefs, tablecloths, knitted gloves and socks, dresses, real dresses that you could wear, and all made by children no older than fourteen.

Then there were the boys' exhibits, even more astounding, wireless sets that really worked, stools, small tables, fire-screens, all as good as in the shops, and all made by those big, rough boys who terrorised us outside the school premises.

Each year at the end of the Christmas term it was the tradition at our school for each class to present a short play for the enjoyment of all the pupils. In my first year at big school the staff decided that as the class plays were unusually good that year they were worth repeating as a public concert in the Corn Exchange. This must have entailed a great deal of hard work for the teachers. Costumes and scenery had to be transported, and few of them had cars. Our teachers came to school on foot, or on bicycles. They must also have had considerable worry about the cast, sent home from school at four o'clock and told to turn up at the back of the Corn Exchange at six-thirty. None of us were on the phone, and one missing Wise Man could have ruined the drama!

Our class had produced a play called 'Santa's Helpers', and I was Fairy Holly, in green gauze and a crown of thorns. My wand was beautiful beyond belief, thickly wound round with red, green and silver tinsel which sparkled in the electric light with a more than earthly radiance. I cannot remember being nervous, but was more excited than ever before.

Daddy was in the audience, although I could not see him. I waited in the wings for my entrance, listening for my cue. The two little 'sleepy-heads' in pyjamas were lying wide-eyed in the bed. Fairy Snowflake had entered, stepping over the low sill of the unglazed pseudo-window, standing by the head of the bed with her back to the window and facing the audience according to plan.

This was my moment to skip across to the bed and declaim -

> 'I am Fairy Holly.
> You have no need to fear.
> I only come to warn you
> That Santa Claus is near' -

then to take down the stockings and lay them on the table ready for Father Christmas.

I was poised with one foot raised ready to take off when a pair of hands descended on my shoulders, and a voice in my ear whispered,

"Blow the candle out."

This was not in my brief. In total surprise I turned and looked into teacher's face.

"Blow out the candle," she repeated, indicating its position with her head, quite unnecessarily. I knew where the candle was.

It had been the job of one of the little sleepy-heads to place it, lighted, on the pseudo-window sill, where in the cross draughts of the stage it had developed a high and exploring flame. By now it was wavering perilously close to the gauzy wings of Fairy Snowflake, who was correctly stationed just in front of it. I saw what teacher meant. Yes, it would have to be blown out. I set off quickly towards the point of danger, using the normal method of locomotion.

"Don't walk. Skip."

Of course, I ought to have thought of that! Pretend it's part of the play. I skipped to the candle and blew, bending close to make certain of quick success. In bending over, my wand, so perfectly tutored to the expected, poked upwards behind me and uncrowned Fairy Snowflake. A very wide-awake sleepy-head leaned dangerously out of bed to retrieve the glittering tiara, which Fairy Snowflake replaced at a rakish angle. I skipped back and hid for a moment in the wings as before, then went into my full routine according to the script.

When the curtains came down we all crowded round our teacher, elated and relieved.

"Well done." she said. "It was lovely, except for Jane, who was clumsy."

I blushed, and had no answer.

"I asked you to do a simple thing, and you messed it up. But the rest of you did very well."

My evening was spoilt. I was very near to tears. I had been so confident, and so enthusiastic about it all. My greatest wish had been to make our play the best, and I had unintentionally failed them. I was too young to realise that, ashamed of her own lack of foresight, the teacher had eased her mortification by means of a scapegoat.

"Did you like our play, Daddy? Was it good?"

"Very good. I liked your play the best."

"Teacher said I spoilt it because I was clumsy. But it wasn't really in the play, not that blowing the candle out. I wasn't supposed to do that, but teacher told me to."

"You weren't clumsy, my dear. You did it very well. It was lovely, all lovely."

I had a presentiment that my teacher would hold an inquest upon our performance, and went to school the next morning with a heavy heart. I was right, but it was not as bad as I had feared. The headmistress came in and congratulated all the children on their acting.

"Your little accident was a pity, Jane, but not really your fault. You weren't expecting to have to blow the candle out, were you?"

"No."

Her words, and Daddy's, restored my spirits and my damaged confidence, and also gave me an early insight into the hazards of treading the boards.

As the family grew up we sometimes took our picnics on Greenham Common instead of at Enborne. This was rather a long walk including a climb up Pyle Hill, but it was well worth the effort once we were there. Before the Second World War this common land was one of Newbury's amenities, a beauty spot of inestimable value. There were acres of open heath, covered with gorse, heather and bracken, mossy walks, flat stretches for ball games, pine trees for climbing and shade, blackberries for gathering, rushes for weaving into little baskets, tiny blue fritillaries and harebells for them to alight upon.

When in 1941, the U.S.A.A.F. moved into Greenham there was a public understanding, supported by the press, that the land would be restored to local use after the war. This never happened, although there was a time when it fell into partial disuse, and we were able to walk on crumbling runways and watch Nature churning up the concrete. It served one temporary purpose after another until, in 1953 a new, fast piece of road was built from the Newtown Road at the 'Swan', and the old road which had been so familiar to us was suddenly sealed by an enormous pair of gates. It seemed like a door being slammed in one's face. There was no longer any hopes of the people of Newbury getting back any of their common rights.

My family always preferred to walk a little farther across the common to a part called Peckmore. It was a private estate with a public footpath running through it. Here we found fewer people, and could play at hide-and-seek without accidentally finding someone else's brother or sister. After the long walk we were always hungry and thirsty, so the packed meal was our first pleasure.

"I'm going to walk about with mine. Can we, Mamma?"

"Yes, if you want to. But I thought you were tired."

"I'm not now. I want to go exploring. Are you coming, Lucy?"

Lucy was, and Peter, and Norma. We all went together, running up each little opening and back, delighted to be free, afraid of getting lost. Meals at home were highly disciplined affairs, so it was a novelty to run about, sandwich in hand. We returned to base at frequent intervals for re-fuelling, but not until every crumb was consumed, and the lemonade bottle empty did we seriously begin to play.

No picnic, of course, was complete without the camera. It seemed to pop up everywhere. We were able to ignore it, which was what Daddy wanted us to do. I found the shiny eye trained upon me when I was hiding in a clump of heather.

"Don't give me away, will you Daddy? I don't want Lucy to find me."

Click.

"All right, my dear. She's miles away over there. Listen!"

He was right. Away past the pine trees where Mamma was teaching Doreen to walk I heard the hide-and-seek password -

'If you don't holla I shan't folla!'

"Cuckoo." I called, the standard reply.

Lucy heard it and half turned, standing almost shoulder high in green bracken. Her face had that serious, slightly nervous look which meant that she was feeling lonely. I called again.

"Cuckoo."

Then she knew the direction, and her worried expression changed to an eager smile. She plunged through the bracken, past the pine tree 'home' and into the hidden path edged on both sides with heather and ling.

"Got you both," she breathed, flopping down beside Daddy.

"Isn't this a pretty place to hide?" I asked her.

"Mm."

"If you were asked to plant a garden, to plan it and lay it out," Daddy said, "you could not do it as well as this, which grew naturally. This is like a gentleman's garden."

Having for the moment exhausted our immense energy in playing hide-and-seek, Lucy and I wandered about picking reeds from a dried out patch of marshy grass. They were the thin, round type, dark green and smooth, with a sweet, fresh scent. Mamma said,

"You could make a little basket with those."

"How? Will you show us?"

Lucy and I sat down cross-legged and facing each other, knees touching. We held one reed at each end in our teeth, leaving our hands free to work. Other reeds were then twisted and knotted round it at right angles, until a good area of net was stretched between us. Then the reed ends on either side were tied together with a separate reed, and the 'starter' was knotted to form a handle. An attractive little basket was the result.

"Wouldn't it be lovely for easter eggs?"

Easter had gone and I knew it, but there was no harm in planting seed.

The day had cooled, and Mamma was clearly getting packed up for the long homeward walk. Reluctantly we turned our faces toward the road, not only tired, but as always on our outings, desperately thirsty. There was one thing to be grateful for. Having walked up Pyle Hill in the morning, we were now walking down it. I cried quietly in bed that night, haunted by the dreadful loneliness during the dark hours, of that lovely spot. It seemed to have a sentient life, capable of being hurt by our careless desertion after the rapturous enjoyment of the day.

There were some occasions, when we were a little older, when Laura and Jeanie would go on their own to Greenham Common, and would invite Lucy and me to join them. They came to call for us, each holding a handle of the bag which contained their sandwiches and bottle. With their stiffly-whitened tennis shoes, clean ankle socks and starched cotton dresses I thought they looked too posh to go for a picnic. I was quite different being on the common without parents or any adult. We stayed nearer to the road edge, away from the pine trees, and played ball games most of the time, rounders, pig-in-the-middle, Queenie, and endless variations of French Cricket. We ate our own food, and never exchanged any. It would have seemed to me disloyal to have done so. They too had only one bottle of lemonade. It was so heavy to carry. Although Lucy and I had half a bottle each instead of a fifth we were still tortured with thirst long before we needed to start for home. There was, however, an oasis. Set in a slight hollow among the bracken was a house called 'The Ark', where lived a kindly couple whose name we never did discover. Deperate children knocking at the back door would, if they made the request

Making a rush basket

Our road flooded

Mamma hangs out the wash

Photo by Hawker & Son.]

THE COUNTY GIRLS' SCHOOL, NEWBURY.

Newbury County Girls' School

politely, be given a glass of water, or even two. I am sure they got fed up with opening their door and watching children gulp water, but there must be quite a few people still living in Newbury who are grateful to Mr. and Mrs. Noah for saving so many young lives threatened by dehydration.

CHAPTER THIRTEEN

When Lucy and I went to Sunday School our favourite route was by the canal. Peeling off left from Craven Road we went along Kennet Road which brought us right up to the towpath, with the weavers' cottages on our left. These cottages were very poor and tumbledown places when we were children. Now they are fully restored and modernised, and are very desirable residences. We crossed the wooden bridge and walked along the towpath on the other side, until we came to the little, low wooden bridge where the canal meets the River Kennet. This bridge was a ricketty affair of rotting planks, and the widening spaces between them allowed us alarming glimpses of swift water below. In rough weather it was often partially flooded, and Lucy and I had the choice of wet shoes all the afternoon, or a long walk retracing our steps. We were both a little nervous of this creaking, deteriorating structure.

"In fifty years," Lucy told me, "I shan't come this way any more."

I was inclined to agree, or even to shorten her set time.

That old bridge has long been replaced by a less picturesque, but more serviceable metal footbridge, and raised above the flooding level.

For many years the canal was in a state of neglect. It was no longer needed for the transport of coal into and out of the Wharf, and the modern adaptation to pleasure cruising had not then begun. It was sluggish in flow, smelly, and choked with weeds. One year dredgers were sent to clear the canal, as there was a risk of flooding. Tons and tons of black, slimy stinking weed were scraped up and dumped on the towpath, where it lay rotting for many months.

These dredgers finally disposed of the old barge, which had been a familiar sight to me from my earliest days. This barge had been tied up to the island which divided the water between the bridges into two streams, one stream going on under Newbury's ancient and lovely bridge, the other flowing swiftly down to the Hovis Mill. Each year the boat lost a little more of its blue and red paint, each year it sank a little lower in the water, while the undisturbed rushes grew around it, dab-chicks played in and out of its rotting timbers, and in time it made an attractive picture, with the medieval church of St. Nicholas in the background.

With the water so murky and evil-smelling, the lock became a place of terror. The deep drop between sheer, dark walls, the uncontrolled leakage under pressure through rotted wood, and the scummy filth which collected on the high side were all nightmare material to me. I could imagine no worse fate than to fall far down between those slimy, green walls into the black, unfathomable water. This lock has been recently cleaned and repaired, so for the first time I was really able to see the bottom. It was not unfathomable, as my imagination had made it, but at seven years old it took great courage to cross that lock, walking on the narrow ledge, even when holding the bar. One had to, of course, as the big ones were all doing it.

Sometimes we decided to walk on the other side of the canal, along West Mills and past the Parish Church. This part of the canal has now been deflected, and flats are being built on the island. Previously the water rushed under the mill platform, turning the huge wheel which powered the Hovis works. This also was a little frightening in its demonstration of the weight and force of water. The flour mill was open on one side, so it was possible to see the men at their work, their hair and shoes white as their coats. The sacks of flour, when filled, were sent down a chute at the roadside for convenient loading onto lorries. It was a busy, noisy, interesting place to stand and stare.

We had a friend called Brenda, who lived in Russell Road, where the houses all have long, narrow gardens running up to the towpath. Brenda's was a lovely garden, full of flowers, fruit, vegetables, with a little gate at the far end. In winter these gardens were sometimes flooded, but when the water subsided the soil seemed to be the richer for it. Going to tea with Brenda was a delight, once the peril of Jock was overcome. Jock was a wire-haired terrier and a good house-dog, which meant that he resented visitors and made it next to impossible for them to get into the house. Lucy and I were both nervous of Jock, but Brenda's Mamma soon quietened him, and made him lie down in his basket, where he would produce alternating snores and growls all the time we were there.

Brenda's Mamma always gave us jelly for our tea, and fancy cakes. The cakes were the very kind I liked best, halfpenny ones from Roberts's. Brenda had them often. Brenda was an only child. Her Mamma always scrambled the jelly with a fork, which seemed to me regrettable. It seemed such a waste of beauty, such a waste of that unbroken transparency which I found irresistibly fascinating. Certainly the scrambled jelly was easier to manage, and it tasted just as nice.

As an extra treat during the consumption of these goodies we listened to a story told by Uncle Mac on the wireless, a new acquisition which almost, but not quite, saw me falling into covetousness. Wouldn't it be lovely, all day to have wonderful stories pouring out of that big trumpet? I hope they ask us to tea again soon. I like sitting on a cushion to have my tea. I wonder why we haven't got any cushions.

There were chickens in Brenda's garden, and we were allowed to help collect the eggs.

"How do they lay eggs?"

Everyone knew that hens laid eggs, but no-one had explained the process by which.

Brenda's Mamma laid a finger on her lips.

"Sh! Come here. I'll tell you."

We stepped conspiratorially into the house, and she whispered in my ear.

"It's just like us going to the toilet, but don't talk about it, will you pet?"

When the untalked-about eggs were all collected we went fishing. Lucy and I had brought our fishing nets from home, so we all filed up the path, through the little gate and onto the towpath. We wandered along, making a minute survey of the water until we found a shoal of minnows close enough to the side for us to reach. As we slid the net underneath them of course, they all darted away, neatly keeping their relative positions unchanged in full 3D, a marvel to me. Then came a test of patience, and of physical control, because the least movement of the net sent the returning minnows arrowing away again. When they had foolishly decided that the net was harmless it was firmly lifted clear of the water, and with luck one or two little silver bodies would be seen threshing about in the net in panic. We always supposed that as soon as we got them into the jam-jar they were perfectly happy, especially as we always gave them a couple of inches of Canadian Pondweed to make them feel at home.

Sticklebacks were a status symbol. The child who could show off with one of these in his jar was embarked upon a career of one-upmanship. On one of our early fishing expeditions we learned in an unforgettable way that tadpoles and sticklebacks together in a jar are evolution in action, the stickleback being the fitter for survival, in jam-jars. But the absolute king among infant fishermen was the one who could land a stony gudgeon. These fish, with their grey bodies pressed flat against

51

the stones and mud in the shallow water looked delightfully easy prey. But as we prodded underneath them we raised a cloud of mud, under cover of which they shot away unseen. Brenda, Lucy and I tried and tried again. But when it was time to go home our jars contained nothing more than a few fragile, darting minnows.

"No, you can't bring them indoors." Mamma was firm about this, so we put them on the outside windowsill to spend a comfortable night. By morning they were swimming a little drunkenly, showing first one silver flank and then the other. By the afternoon they had quietly turned onto one side and died. We couldn't understand it, after all our care. It was ungrateful, we felt.

My fear of falling into the canal was almost phobic. I could not bear to see Peter or Norma or Doreen stooping on the edge to look for fish. Daddy did not seem anxious.

"What are you so worried about, my dear? If one of the little ones fell in I'd just put my hand in, like that and pull them out."

That was a partial comfort, but supposing Daddy was not there, or supposing they fell in the lock, or suppose no-one knew they had fallen in. Suppose, suppose . . .

Today the canal is less sinister. Throughout the summer season holiday barges and small pleasure craft dot it with colour and noise. The rotted wood has been replaced and the locks function efficiently. Sedentary fishermen line the towpath with an array of expensive equipment, and the canal has a new and different life. But on dark dull days as I walk there alone I cannot feel that all its threat is lifted.

CHAPTER FOURTEEN

When Lucy had her ninth birthday Mamma and Daddy bought her a book called 'The Golden Annual for Girls'. She enjoyed it, and as soon as I had the chance I read it too. It seemed to me the most exciting book I have ever read. There were boarding-school stories, ghost stories, animal stories, poems and articles, a veritable feast of reading. As my own birthday approached I asked my mother if I could have a 'Golden Annual' of my own, as of course the next year's edition would be out. My birthday came, and there was a flat parcel by my breakfast plate. I ripped off the paper in high anticipation and found that I had been given 'The Happy Hours Annual'.

"Aren't you going to say 'Thank you' dear?"

"Yes, thank you very much. I wanted the Golden Annual like Lucy had."

"I know, but there wasn't one. They're not printing any more. I think you'll like that one when you start to read it."

They must have been aware of my disappointment, although I tried not to show it. It was time for school, so I had to leave my new book at home and set out. During the morning I thought about it a great deal. The hard cover, although not golden, was brightly coloured and very shiny. There was a picture of an aeroplane coming down which looked promising, and some poems; I was sure there were poems. I felt quite eager to get home for a second look at my new book.

That evening I read it almost through, and found it delightful. The stories were intricate and engrossing, an advance on all my previous volumes. There were narrative poems, quite long ones, some of them funny and some moving. An unusual feature of that particular book was a series of very brief articles on meanings and derivations of words. Anecdotes and riddles filled tiny printers' crevices, and the whole work was abundantly illustrated. I was totally absorbed, and my initial disappointment had evaporated before the day was out. It was sad to have reached the end, but all was there to be read again and again. Before long I knew the poems by heart, and was able to recite them at the Sunday School party.

"Do you know which is my favourite story in this book, Mamma?"

"No. You tell me."

"A Fortunate Mishap." (The story with the aeroplane).

"A Fortunate what?"

"Mishap."

"Let me see." She put down her knitting and took the book.

"Oh, mis-hap! It's pronounced 'mis-hap', although, yes, it does look like mishap."

"What does it mean?"

"It means a misfortune, something which accidentally goes wrong."

"I thought it was, but it was a good story even when I didn't know."

"Are you pleased with your birthday present?"

"It's the best book I've ever had. It's quite a hard book."

I treasured it for years, and it was in course of time enjoyed by Norma and Doreen as well. Our stock of books was not large, but by pooling our resources we could always find something to read, and we never minded reading favourite stories many times.

As for most children, Christmas to us was the great, glad time of the year. We all believed implicitly in Santa Claus who came down chimneys with a sack filled with toys. Even the jolly pictures in books which showed him and his sack about three times the width of the chimney he was entering could not shake our faith, and the joy of anticipation at bedtime on Christmas eve was often accompanied by a nervous stomach-ache at the thought of his getting into our bedroom. Our parents assured us that no-one ever saw him, and we had no need to worry.

One thing I quickly learned about Santa Claus was his strong tendency to have favourites, not within families, but between them. Whilst we were gleefully un-earthing nuts and sweets from the toes and heels of Daddy's woollen socks, Laura and Jeanie and others whom we knew were straddling new bikes which had some-how been manoeuvred down the chimney, or pushing new shiny dollies' prams with big new dolls smartly outfitted in lovely pink wool. I could not see wherein these children had been more virtuous than we. They occasionally told lies, and often said 'daft'. The funny thing was that Santa Claus took these fine new toys to children who already had one. Laura and Jeanie both had a bike, which seemed good enough for anyone, but Santa Claus brought them each a new and better model. We had none at all, and would have welcomed one of their old ones, but these had mysteriously disappeared.

We were not a family to sleep late in the morning, especially on Christmas morning. At five-thirty Lucy and I were awake and whispering quietly. Too early yet to wake the others. Let's count a thousand. One, two, three, four, five. It was surprising how quickly it could be done. Another look at the clock, (brought up from the living-room by kind permission, a safeguard against our waking the little ones in the small hours). Another thousand, and say the alphabet, the months, and all the tables we knew. Six o'clock! It was now permitted to get up.

Lucy lit the little paraffin lamp on the shelf. I undid the bottom of our double bed, and we both crept into the other room to fetch Peter and Norma. They brought their pillows with them and got in at the end of our bed. Lucy picked up Doreen from her cot and sat her between her two big sisters. Christmas had begun.

A rolled-up colouring book, a pair of knitted mittens, a puzzle with little balls to be rolled into slots, a paper screw of sweets, four big festive ones, not the kind to be bought with a Saturday penny. More like the ones in the 'International Stores' called 'Ritz Assortment'. An apple, red and foreign, an orange, and some wholly unassailable nuts in their shells. The basic goodies were the same for each of us. It was just in the matter of little toys that Santa Claus had used his dis-cretion. This year Peter had a drum, Lucy and I had a dulcimer each, and Doreen and Norma a small doll. There was little chance for our parents to have a quiet lie-in, with five of us chattering excitedly, playing musical instruments and filling the bed with orange peel and paper.

Our first home Christmas tree was a revelation to me. Lucy and I had seen one at the Sunday School party the previous year, but this was different. It was of course smaller, but big enough to allow me to stoop underneath and look up into it. I was in an entire little green world, seeing what would have been seen by birds who might have slept in it. The mystery and magic were enhanced by the glass baubles and tinsel, the tiny candles in holders, and the intoxicating, resinous smell.

Each evening during Christmas Daddy used to turn the gas-light low and a ring of bright eyes would watch him go through the slow ritual of lighting the candles. After a few minutes we were all allowed to blow them out, loving and hating the waxy smell which hung around the room.

When Lucy and I went to the Sunday School party I noticed that their candles were not lit, for the second year in succession. I asked the teacher why,

"Well, you see, it wouldn't be safe, would it? The tree might catch fire."

"Ours never catches fire at home."

"No, well, your Mum and Dad are there to see to it. Anyway, the candles will do for next year if we don't light them."

True. But such a perpetuation of non-fulfillment seemed to me very like falsehood. I could not approve.

The lack of tree lights was wholly forgotten however when the time came for the distribution of gifts. The teachers arranged all the little chairs in two rows facing each other down the length of the hall, and we all sat down.

"Now, children, we have a special visitor waiting to come and see us. Can you all be very, very quiet?"

"It's Father Christmas." Lucy whispered in my ear, before silence fell like a cloak over all. She was an experienced party-goer.

All the hall lights were switched off, leaving only the glow of the huge coal fire, closely guarded by a nursery fireguard and all the helpers. A faint and distant tinkle of bells was heard, and the far door opened. Framed in the doorway stood Santa Claus in all his impractical chimney-going gear, and his two fairies in spotless white and silver, with huge wings which had certainly had no contact at any time with soot. Santa Claus held each fairy by the hand and they moved slowly between the two ranks of chairs to stand before the Christmas tree. His speech to the children was short, we were pleased to find, and the distribution of gifts began. Each present was named, and as our name was called we walked up to accept it and to say 'thank you'. The ceremony began in obedient silence, but as more and more children had had and opened their presents the chattering grew louder and louder, until Santa Claus had difficulty in making his voice heard. My gift at my first party was a necklace of brown beads, graded in size and sparkling, which I wore every day for weeks. The following year I was given a small doll with dark hair, to which I gave the name of Bella. Walking home from the party, very proudly and carefully, I was tripped up by a dog in Craven Road. It rushed out of a gateway headlong in front of me and down we went, Bella and I, and her pretty face was smashed to pieces. She had not even reached home in safety! I have never much cared for dogs.

The time came when it was Lucy's turn to be a fairy, and a little later I was chosen. The total routine had become institutionalised, but the successive groups of children enjoyed it afresh each year.

A few days after my sixth Christmas when Mamma was doing the washing she said to Lucy and me,

"Look what I found in your stockings, right in the toes, a nice hanky each."

We thanked her, wondering how we could have missed them.

"She didn't find them in our stockings." I told Lucy.

"You don't know. She might have."

But I did know. I had turned that woollen sock inside out and investigated the woolly stuff in the top of the toe. Not even a silver threepenny bit could have escaped detection! I was left with the disturbing discovery of parental mendacity. Mamma had lied to us. She had lied to protect the Santa Claus legend, to protect our happiness. It was a moment for taking stock of moral priorities, for catching a glimpse of a gap between truthfulness and literalness.

CHAPTER FIFTEEN

We were, I suppose, a fairly musical family. Both our parents had been choir members, in fact their first meeting was in the Choir vestry at Northbrook Street Church. My mother and several of her sisters had sung in the choir for a number of years.

Just before the First World War my father, having completed his apprenticeship in Devon, found work in Newbury with a firm of builders. He was by trade a carpenter and joiner. Naturally on a Sunday his footsteps turned towards the Methodist Church, and he was soon asked to join the choir, where he saw, and fell in love with, my pretty mother.

When war broke out he was among the first to be called up, as a 'sapper' in the Royal Engineers. By this time he had a charming little daughter, Lucy, and was, I'm certain, very reluctant to leave wife and child and embark for France. Having been trained to respect authority, he undoubtedly did his duty, whatever it was and wherever it lay, but he was not an enthusiastic soldier. This I have deduced from the fact that he rarely talked about his army days, unlike many men of his generation who talked of nothing else. Not from him did we hear of the excitements and the glamour of war. He was interested in the arts of peace, of which music was one.

As a boy he had chosen to play the violin. It was, he claimed, the most expressive of all instruments, the nearest approach to the human voice. He had bought quite a good violin, and had worked on it over the years, adjusting the bridge, smoothing the pegs, and even applying a special type of varnish to the back. He once changed the sound-post for one slightly thicker to improve the tone, a ticklish operation. I watched him, and he explained what he was trying to do. The old post had to be removed, which was not difficult, and the new one introduced and set upright, fitting tightly against the belly and the back of the instrument. This could only be done by working through the scroll-shaped holes on either side of the bridge. With loops of wire and string, and hours of finicky manipulation he at last pulled it into an upright position, and it worked.

We were always deeply interested in Daddy's violin, or 'fiddle', as he called it. It gave off excitingly vibrant sounds when we plucked the strings, and a unique, resinous resistance as we slid our fingers up and down them. The black wooden case was lined with royal blue baize, and fitted with several little containers, shaped to the outline of the instrument. When we lifted the lids of these we found within spare strings, a mute, a piece of resin in a tin, a bridge. The bow was lodged inside the lid, and kept in place by two turn-buttons. The whole outfit, as we bent over to investigate with our faces almost inside, had a shut-in, violiny smell not met with anywhere else.

Daddy always looked funny to me when he played his fiddle. I think it was the chin-rest which seemed odd, and I have still the same feeling now when watching violinists on television. He usually started by running off a few scales in various keys, and then began on his pieces, of which he had a good repertoire. His best practice time was when we were all in bed, and we frequently fell asleep to the thin wail of the violin playing Wagner, Mendelssohn or Mozart.

Sometimes he made a mistake, or was very slightly off pitch, and knowing this, he used to stop and put it right, then having done so he would go over the little phrase a dozen or more times, until we were driven to cover our heads with our little calico nighties to deaden some of the sound.

We, in our turn, used to drive Mamma round the bend with those dulcimers, brought by Santa Claus via the chimney-pot. There was no piano in our house, but we were all so piano-mad that friends and relatives who invited us to tea had often locked their pianos and unfortunately mislaid the key before we arrived.

This had happened one Sunday afternoon when we went to tea with Newbury Grandma at her Craven Road house.

Pity, I thought. I wonder if it is really locked.

By trying the lid I proved it really to be so. Then I remembered seeing a small key popped into a vase on the mantelshelf. I had a quick look and there it was, just the right size for that little hole.

"Here it is, Grandma. I've found it. It was in your little vase."

But where was all the gratitude and praise due to me?

"Just you go and put it back where you found it, and leave it there, there's a good girl."

I was slowly getting the measure of the adult mind. This was one more little lesson, an insight into the thresholds of tolerance, white lying, expediency.

The dulcimers were the nearest thing to musical instruments that came our way. Each was in a neat box with a lid, and a little wooden mallet fitted into the slot at the side. The ten silver bars, so highly polished, and so well worth a frequent rub-up with a hanky, looked good enough for a seraphim to play in heaven. The bars were lettered, C D E F, another F with noughts and crosses by it, another B with a small b by it, right up to a short little C and beginning again. It would have simplified things for Lucy and me had they gone straight through from A to J, but in battling with a properly named keyboard we learned a great deal.

"Lucy, listen to mine. I'm playing 'Away in a Manger'."

"That's not right. You haven't got 'crib' right."

"Well, I can't help it. It plays that note. You try."

She did, and she got 'crib' wrong. She gave a tap on the B with a small b by it. "Ah, that's it. Listen."

Slowly she went through the tune, using the B flat, and it was perfect.

I copied, and we played and sang together.

The same problem arose with 'Once in Royal', but we discovered that by using the F with the noughts and crosses by it the funny-sounding interval was corrected.

We picked out many of our songs and carols and hymns in this way, since fortunately much of the music written for children is in the simple keys of C, G and F.

"We must make a music book, then we can play together without making mistakes."

I agreed, since it was annoying to find, each time we played in unison, that either one or the other of us made a mistake, and spoiled the performance. There was the usual hunt for writing-paper, and scissors, and pencils, and a needle and cotton to stitch the pages, and a picture for the cover, and paste with which to stick it, all of which passed happy hours for us both, and then we were ready to write the notes. This was simple. Since we had evolved no way of indicating the time or rhythm of the tunes, our music books simply directed us on pitch, and it did eliminate most of the mistakes. Peter and Norma soon learned to play tunes by using our books, and as we taught them some of the words we could all sing together. Even little Doreen, who was two, loved singing, and often made up songs of her own, which were a kind of recitative of all the things she had recently been doing. The trouble was in bringing her songs to an end.

For quality of sound Peter's drum might just as well have been a toffee tin with a string through it, but it was painted in drum colours and had a leather strap and two drumsticks, all of which gave it a martial authenticity. Being now a three-instrument family, with four vocalists and a baby the obvious next step was to produce a concert. Lucy and I had had school concert experience and were full of ideas. We were helped by the fact that it was Christmas time, and the festive mood was still with us, and also that there was a supply of decorative material not available at other times of the year. We set to work.

Music and singing were to be the main element in our concert, and our carols were already well practised. Doreen, who wanted to sing with us had to be excluded, but we promised her that she could be a fairy and sing a song by herself.

"With a wand?"

"Yes, of course." She was satisfied.

We invited our parents to our concert, which was to take place after tea that evening. They gladly accepted, and at the appointed time took their seats on two wooden chairs, an audience of two, all we needed.

We began with carols, accompanied by two dulcimers, a tin drum, and several mistakes. Having decided whose fault it was, and argued a bit, we did the verse again and got it right.

"Now let's have just one verse without the instruments, shall we, so we can hear your voices?"

"Daddy, you're not supposed to talk, because we're up on the stage."

"All right. I won't any more, if you'll sing me one verse."

We did, as an insurance against further interruptions, and then proceeded after some discussion about costumes, with the next item of the programme, the 'Balloon Dance'.

This of course had been suggested to us by the availability of balloons at the time. Only Lucy and I took part, as the little ones could not be relied upon to catch a balloon once it had left their hands. Our music was little random taps on the tin drum by Peter, but we danced our dance regardless of all else, pointing our toes in their thick, tartan-patterned button-up carpet slippers, pirouetting and bending, throwing and catching our balloons with the dedicated intentness of ballerinas, and all on a piece of brown lino four feet long and three feet wide. Our parents clapped as loudly as an audience of two could.

Now it was Doreen's turn. Interval, whilst we dressed the fairy, according to promise. We put both our tinsel crowns on her head, gave her a stick wound round with tinsel, and fastened tree decorations to her slippers with my elastic garters. No wings, as they were too difficult to make. She looked adorable, and was intensely earnest about it all. She trotted onto centre stage.

"Doreen, here a minute. Let me take your pinny off."

That done, the little fairy commenced to steal the limelight. In a free-flowing plain-song she related how she had had some Christmas cake for tea, but "I don't like it, I like the icing but not that yellow stuff. I don't like Daddy's ginger, it burns my mouth, well I like the juice, and Father Christmas gave me a dolly and some big sweets and, I forget, and an orange . . ."

We let her rattle on for a few minutes and then suggested that that was enough. She ignored her older sisters and sang on and on and on. Lucy took her gently by the hand.

"Come on. Doreen, you've finished your song."

"I haven't." She snatched her hand away and rolled into part two. A few more minutes passed and we were getting bored. The hint of a smile twitched my mother's lips.

"Doreen, I want to see your wand, and your crown." She picked her up and sat her on her knee. "Now I can have a good look at my fairy."

There were no tears. We moved gratefully into our final item, a group of carols and songs with full instrumentation and no interference from the audience. Our concert had been a great success.

CHAPTER SIXTEEN

When Lucy was ten years old she won a scholarship to Christ's Hospital. Newbury is endowed with a number of such scholarships through the generosity of John and Francis West, who left money, back in the seventeenth century in trust for the education of poor boys and girls, preference being given to their own kin.

Lucy's scholarship caused quite a stir at home because it was unexpected. The six places vacant in September had not been taken up, so an extra examination was held to find suitable entrants and Lucy was selected. This meant that she started at Christ's Hospital in January instead of September.

There were certain health formalities, such as vaccination and dental checks, and a trunk had to be procured. It all happened fairly quickly. In no time at all, it seemed, Christmas was over, and a tearful Lucy was being seen into the train in her best clothes.

There was a sudden loneliness at home. Peter was the only boy, and as such held a special place. Norma and Doreen were close in age and good playmates. I was now the elder sister, and yet not. I never admitted to loneliness, and resented being questioned about it, but an irreplaceable part of my life was gone. Lucy and I had been inseparable, and whilst I was missing our close, relaxed companionship, Lucy was missing the whole family life which she loved.

Soon after the day of separation a large parcel arrived at our home. It contained Lucy's home clothes, every single garment, woollen socks, cotton dress, knickers and petticoat made at home and exactly like my own, her brown laced shoes and fawn coat, all neatly folded and wrapped in the brown paper and string which had been bought in Newbury and taken to school as requested. I had not realised that the uniform included underclothes. It made the rift seem even greater. Mamma was upset, although she did not know that I knew. To me it was another experience of the world's belittlement. Those clothes, paid for with effort and provided in love, were now not good enough. What is Lucy wearing? I wondered. How will it change her?

"What will you do with them, Mamma?"

"Put them away, of course, ready for when she comes home." The slight asperity in her voice was a cloak for her only-just-controlled feelings.

There was an aura of anxiety surrounding the family which I could sense, being now the oldest child at home. Friends took us out, or invited us to tea after school more often than was normal, and on some occasions more often than I liked. There was another baby on the way, of which fact we were of course completely ignorant. This in itself was a reason for concern, but the worry was increased by our mother's deteriorating health. There was no-one at home with whom I could discuss my anxiety, and I was never willing to discuss family affairs with my friends.

I worked my way up into Standard Four. School was my security in a sea of uncertainty. Lucy was no longer there, and some of the girls pestered me with questions about Christ's Hospital which I really could not answer. Even the teachers each asked me the same questions separately. However, there was plenty to learn, and I was happy to learn well. This was fortunate, as I could not have faced school failure as well as my home anxieties.

The year wore itself on. Lucy came home at Easter, but she did not put on her home clothes like mine. She wore her school clothes all the time, and did not look like Lucy. Neither did she sound like Lucy. Her Berkshire accent had dropped away, and we had to get used to the neat, clipped speech of the Christ's Hospital girls.

"Don't make comments," I was told. "It wouldn't hurt you to take a little more care with your speech. You're terribly broad."

"I thought broad meant wide."

"So it does, usually, but in speech it means that you have got too much of the local accent."

"Well, Lucy talks broad Christ's Hospital and no-one seems to mind."

"That'll do. Remember what I say."

Lucy and I quickly picked up our old friendship and were happy in the holidays, although something of the old relationship had gone for ever. She told me everything I wanted to know about her new school. I learned all the names of the girls in her ward, and all their quirks, until I felt that I too knew them.

The spartan regime did not worry her much. We were used to it at home, and Lucy never complained of the food or conditions of living. But on going away day the tears began to flow at the breakfast table, rising to a flood by the time of her departure. I was always glad when that day was over.

During the long summer holiday it almost seemed to me that we got back onto the old footing. Lucy put on her own cotton dresses, and her plimsolls; we did the old familiar things, and I had got used to her different way of talking. I was still avid for all her school news. She taught me a number of the hymns used in 'chapel', and the songs from her singing classes. There were also some school traditional songs which I learned,

'Jolly C. H. girls are we, etc.'

and the breaking up song -

'No more Latin, no more French;
'No more sitting on a hard old bench.
No more basins, no more jugs,
No more filthy drinking mugs.' etc.

All this was to me a foretaste of life at its fullest, although I was slightly discomfited by what appeared to me an ungrateful attitude in these songs, or a disloyal one, was perhaps nearer to the mark. There was of course only one thing for me to do. I must get to Christ's Hospital myself.

Meanwhile we had a happy summer vacation. We were able to take the little ones out to Greenham Park, and play with them in the garden or on the green. Lucy's friends wanted to see her whilst we were on holiday from school, and we went out to tea quite often. Brenda, and Laura and Jeanie were available for playing. Sometimes we went to the swimming pool and spent long afternoons there. All too soon the bright, hot August was over, and the tearful day of departing had arrived.

Without Lucy to play with I was again a prey to all the anxieties which had been in abeyance for a few carefree weeks. Every adult friend I met asked,

"How's your Mamma, dear?" with deep concern.

"All right, thank you," was my stock reply. It was not true, but I did not know what else to say, and in any case I would not be drawn into a discussion about it. That she was poorly I knew, and I had to do many things to help her. During the term, of course, she had to cope with the two little ones at home all day on her own, but when I was home the best help I could give her was to look after them, and this I normally enjoyed. Norma and Doreen would gladly play house for hours at a time, and Peter, who was six, was quite good as a daddy, going to work and hammering away with his small tool-set at the other end of the room. And we played schools, in which my role as teacher was never questioned.

I was working hard at school, having now an objective in view, to win a scholarship to Christ's Hospital. My parents agreed with me in this.

The traumatic September day, so clearly remembered, was warm and golden. I ran home from school at dinner time, revelling in the transparent sunshine, and found outside an ambulance. My heart gave a wild lurch, and I ran upstairs, meeting Daddy coming down.

"What's up?"

"Up? Nothing's up, my dear. Go out and play a little while, will you? Stay in the garden till I call you."

I did not, could not, go out of the house. Daddy had gone on downstairs, and I went into my bedroom. The door of my parents' room was closed. I was not intended to go in. Standing by my bed, frozen with fear, I just waited and listened. From the big bedroom I could hear a low moaning sound, over and over again. Daddy was clattering some cups downstairs. My mother was alone, and I could stand it no longer. Crossing the landing I lifted my hand to the latch.

"Don't go in there, Jane. I told you to go outside. I don't want you in. Do you understand?"

I started slowly, reluctantly down the stairs, one unwilling foot after another, sliding my hands down the handrail, and listening. Daddy had passed me going up, carrying a cup of hot milk. He went into the bedroom.

"Try and drink a little of this. It will do you good." (That must be the milk.) A sharp little cry from Mamma.

"Oh, fool! What a fool I am! Of course it's hot. I'll cool it with a drop of water."

Into the bathroom. Tap turned on.

"That's better now. Try a little more. That's it."

I had reached the bottom stair and slithered out into the garden. No dinner. No-one to talk to. Where are all the others? I've been standing out here for hours! It must be nearly school time. What shall I do? I'll have to go soon. I'll go in the kitchen and see what the time is.

Daddy was in the kitchen, making cocoa.

"There you are, Jane. Have that now and I'll get something better for our tea."

Cocoa, bread and butter and cheese. I was to consume a lot of these in the next few years.

"Where's Peter, Daddy, and Norma and Doreen?"

"They're all right as rain. Don't you worry. Mrs. Westgate is looking after Peter, and the little girls are with Mrs. South. Get off to school now, and I'll still be here when you come home."

I had not asked the burning question. I knew its answer. Mamma had gone to hospital. Nothing in school interested me that afternoon; I was crushed. I knew as clearly as if it had been printed that things were never going to be the same again.

At home I found Daddy opening a tin of something, and frying potatoes. It smelt good, and both of us were hungry. I watched him scoop out the contents of the tin into a saucepan.

"What kind of beans are they, Daddy?"

"Haricot beans, but they're cooked in tomato sauce, with bits of pork too. Look, it says, 'pork and beans' on the tin."

Those were my very first baked beans, and I thought highly of them. The pork content turned out to be two very thin slices of fat rasher, but bolstered up with fried potatoes it all made a good meal. Fortified with food, I ventured to ask a question.

"How long will Mamma be in the hospital?"

"Not long, we hope. We must wait and see."

"Who's going to look after us?"

"Yes, well, I want to have a talk to you about that. Doreen and Norma have gone to stay with Auntie Rose and Uncle Tom for a week or two, and on Friday Grandma and Grandpa are coming to take you to Devon for a little holiday."

"What, by myself?" Alone on the wide beach, out of season, with darkening evenings, and without the family? The image was alarming!

"What shall I do all by myself?"

"You needn't worry about that. Grandma and Grandpa will take good care of you."

The anxiety I was feeling increased as the strange, short evening wore into darkness, and I went to bed uneasy. By the morning the fear had diminished, and I began to look forward to the unexpected holiday.

Daddy and I lived for the rest of the week on baked beans, corned beef, bread and margarine, cocoa and oranges, and at last it was Friday and we were waiting on the station. I was to travel in the guard's van. The guard was a kindly fellow, with children of his own. He had promised to keep an eye on me and to see me picked up at Kingsbridge station. The train drew out from Newbury station, taking me away from my old life for ever.

The guard had a little tip-up seat in the corner of his van which he kindly lent me for the duration of the journey. Daddy had provided me with a small bottle of milk and three halfpenny cakes, an enviable repast. About two miles out of Newbury and feeling in need of a little refreshment I ate one cake and had a sip or two of milk, replacing the cork tightly and wrapping my remaining supplies carefully in the paper bag. I had promised to be no trouble to the guard, who, it had been pointed out to me, had his work to do, so I sat still on his tiny seat for what seemed hours, then partook of more cakes and ale. The guard talked to me, and I told him I was going to Devon.

"That's just as well, seeing as how."

"Seeing as how what?" I asked.

"Seeing as how that's where the train's going."

He told me about his little boys, and I chatted about my brother and sisters, but not a word about our present troubles, which I have always considered were private. There was plenty to look at through the dirty little window, and the guard lent me a rather sooty comic which his little boy had left behind in the cab. It was almost dark when we arrived at Kingsbridge, and Auntie Anne was there to meet me.

"She's been a real good girl," said the guard. "No trouble at all. Been eating and drinking most of the time."

This seemed a little unfair, as my modest rations had had to last me nearly five hours, but it made Auntie Anne laugh. She gave him a whole half-crown for looking after me, which made me feel highly valued.

"You'll be staying overnight with me, dearie, and Grandma and Grandpa will fetch you in the morning."

I was too tired to wonder who lived where, or why. We went to Auntie Anne's little house behind the fruit shop in Fore Street where we ate supper at a round table with several other people whom I did not know. There was meat and cheese, as well, of course, as fruit in profusion, milk for me and tea for the adults. A jar of home-made pickled onions was passed round the table. I had never tasted a pickled onion, and the spicy smell of them was driving me mad with desire. Just as the jar reached me Auntie Anne said,

"Ooh, not for you dear, at this time of night. You'll be having nightmares. Have a tomato."

It was difficult to get to sleep that night, in a strange bed next to the wall, alone, in a room over the street. I was still awake when the visitors left.

CHAPTER SEVENTEEN

We were up early the next morning. It was sunny and the gulls were calling. I went down to the quay with Auntie Anne to fetch the milk, left there each morning in one of her named cans to be picked up. Every morning the can was washed and left on the quay, to be taken away in the morning when the full one was set down.

"Real fresh country milk! That will do you good," Auntie told me. "Better than that blue-looking stuff you get in the town."

I felt a surge of loyalty towards our kind Mr. Westgate. His milk was not perhaps so creamy, but that was not his fault. Following the thought came a wave of homesickness, the picture of Mamma in hospital, and the family scattered.

Devonshire Grandpa arrived at about two with a horse and cart he had borrowed, to take me to Stowers Hill. He gave me a bristly kiss before stowing me and my small amount of luggage into the cart, along with some shopping, and a gift of fruit from his daughter Anne. I sat beside him as he held the reins, and we ambled off away from the town of Salcombe towards South Sands. Here we turned inland towards Marlborough, climbed a hill and arrived at the bungalow.

Devonshire Grandma kissed me kindly, and provided a tea of bread and butter with stiff, seedy blackberry jam. I could tell at once by her attitude that she would treat me well, but that there would be no spoiling. Grandpa was more lenient, and would have enjoyed doing a little spoiling, but it did not lie with him to organise my life.

There was to be no taking cucumber sandwiches to the beach this time. It was too cold to paddle or bathe, and Grandma made it quite clear that she was not on holiday this time. I spent my long leisure hours out of doors, catching grasshoppers and trying to tame them, (an unrewarding task), picking flowers, trying to catch butterflies with a handkerchief, looking for nuts and blackberries in the private lane. On wet days I passed the time reading the old-fashioned books in Grandma's single bookshelf, 'Master Percy's Punishment', 'Never Say Die' and 'Home from the Wars'. I had no toys of any kind, and no companion, but Grandma was too busy to realise this.

Grandpa did though.

"How would you like to come along o'me, my little maid? I'm going to get some lants down to North Sands."

"Ooh, yes. What are lants, Grandpa?"

"They'm little silver things lives in sand. We use 'em for bait, goin' fishing."

We walked to North Sands, broader and a little less hospitable than South Sands. The sky was grey and lowering, and a damp wind blew across the expanse of empty beach. The tide was out, as it needed to be to catch lants, and the sand was wet and wonderfully patterned with broad, smooth, wave-shaped ripples. We took off our shoes and socks and carrying a spade each, (mine a small wooden one), we dug into the sand wherever we saw a worm-cast. The lants were quick to wriggle away and dig more deeply in, and speed was necessary to pick them out and drop them in the tin.

"How can you catch fish with these, Grandpa?"

"You put them on the hook, and then dangle it in the water. The mackerel eats 'em, and gets caught on the hook."

"Why don't the lants drop off?"

"They can't. You puts your hook through your lant, you see. They would drop off else."

"That must hurt the lants, doesn't it?"

"Never, it doesn't. They can't feel, you see."

I was relieved to hear this.

There was no-one on the beach but us, and we spent a companionable afternoon finding lants, and were out of busy Grandma's way. As we made our way
back across the sands in the gloom of a dull evening I was revising my concept of
'seaside'.

Perhaps it was Grandpa who had the bright idea of inviting his daughter from
Plymouth to come and spend a few days at the bungalow. This visit gave me great
happiness. Auntie Mary was a cheerful young mother with a two-year old baby girl.
Little Joy was something like Doreen, and filled a gap in my life. It was possible,
with Auntie Mary playing as well, to have a few social games, and this brought
release of spirit to a child who, having always been used to playing with others, had
played alone for four weeks. We had a game of hide-and-seek. First I had to seek for
Joy, who had been hidden by her mother. I was baffled for a time. Then I noticed
that Grandma's galvanised bath, which was always hanging on a nail in the wall, was
gently rocking to and fro. Auntie Mary lifted it gently down, and I found the little
girl curled up inside it, and laughing. When it was my turn to hide I concealed
myself among the fuchsia bushes which edged the steps. Hearing Auntie Mary
approaching, holding Joy by the hand and chattering to her, I went through all the
agony and ecstasy of suspense with which the hiding situation was always fraught.
The old magic still worked. When they found me the little girl squealed with
delight. She was a first child, and playing with others was a novelty to her. When
they left to go home to Plymouth it seemed lonelier than ever.

A few days later I discovered a nasty little plot, which had evidently been
hatched between my father and his parents. It seemed to them a good moment,
whilst I was down in Devon alone, to get my tonsils removed. Accordingly we
walked into Salcombe to see Dr. Dan, (so called because there were two brothers
practising in the same town, and to use the surname would have caused confusion).
He was the family doctor, and they requested him to make arrangements. Dr. Dan,
however, demurred, because he discovered a heart murmur, and to my relief the
business was indefinitely postponed.

Whilst in town we visited Auntie Anne in her fruit shop, fragrant with odours
of apples, bananas, oranges, peaches, and huge Victoria plums. She gave me grapes
and asked me what I was doing with myself all day.

"Nothing, really. I go out to play when I've helped Grandma. I've caught heaps
of grasshoppers."

"Haven't you got any toys?"

"No. Mine are all at home."

She rattled in the till and produced one and sixpence.

"You go down to the corner shop and see what you'd like. They sell toys in
that sweet shop. If there's any change you can spend it on sweets."

To one whose income was a penny a week this was riches indeed! Off I went,
quite safely in that small town, out of season. I chose a hoop for sixpence, crayons
and a notebook, and still had a penny or two for sweets. In fact, there was even
change for Auntie Anne. I had a good, big bag of aniseed balls, chosen for their
lasting quality, which, when handed round among the adults proved not very
popular. This had not been done intentionally. It remained a matter of surprise to
me that anyone could dislike any sweet.

Back at the bungalow at Stowers Hill I chose myself a stick and spent a happy evening trundling the hoop down the rough driveway and fetching it up again. No way would it run true, with all those flints to negotiate. Very soon the hoop began to demonstrate a will and a temperament of its own in its journey down the slope, and I started to feel the urge to train it and teach it how to manage. I was not used to utterly silent play.

Grandma came to the door to see whom I was speaking to.

"I'm teaching my hoop to keep straight."

"Well, don't let folks hear you. You know what they say about them as talks to theirselves."

I didn't, and there were no folks to hear me.

September wore on, and a grey, misty October set in. There was less daylight for outdoor play, and little to do indoors. I was filling my note-book with stories about families, and when I could find suitable scraps of paper I drew pictures with the crayons. Our own house was always full of odd bits of paper, but there was no junk in Grandma's house. I missed going out with my hoop, so I talked to it indoors, and told it how to behave.

Auntie Mary and Joy came again, just for the day this time, and as it was a damp day we played indoors. Auntie Mary played on Grandma's piano, and Joy and I sang rhymes and songs and hymns, dancing about the room, delighted to be together again.

Joy was put on my bed for her afternoon rest, and I wandered out to sit on the bench overlooking the harbour, as the mist had lifted a little. The bench was just below the sitting-room window. I heard Auntie Mary come into the room from putting Joy down to rest.

"Do you know, that child's put her hoop in a jumper and sat it on the chair? Have you seen it?"

"She does the queerest things. She talks to it. I've heard her at it. And calls it some name or other. I think she's a bit . . . you know, meself."

"Oh, no Mother, she isn't. She's lonely, that's all. See how happy she is playing with Joy. She's used to a big family, don't forget. You know a lonely child will often have an imaginary playmate, and she's done that with a hoop. How long is she staying?"

"The Lord only knows! She can't go back with her mother still in hospital, and now all these other problems. Could be months."

"Why don't you get her into school? She'd like that, and it would take her off your hands all day."

"We thought of that, only it's so far into Salcombe. We can't go in and back every day."

I jumped off the bench and ran about singing before going indoors. Joy had not slept, and it was time for them to go, so I walked up the driveway with them to the top.

"Are you coming again?"

"I hope so, dear. If we can. Be a good girl for Grandma, won't you?"

They were off, and I walked back slowly, having a great deal to think about.

The next morning, soon after breakfast we all set out for Salcombe. We were going to call on Auntie Anne, and Grandpa had promised to take me on the beach for a little while. We had dinner in the cosy little room behind the shop, and then Grandpa put on his cap and took his walking stick and we set off. South Sands was bleak and grey; gulls swooped threateningly and the small boats at anchor rocked in the shallow water with a sad, abandoned look. No-one else was about.

We had an interesting talk. I drew patterns on the sand and wrote my name with the walking stick. There were some highly desirable shells there for the taking, and Grandpa told me about the moon and the tides. We did not look for lants.

We arrived back at the shop in time for tea, doughnuts and bananas and chocolate biscuits. As soon as we were all seated Auntie Anne said,

"How would you like to go to school, Jane?"

Wide-eyed and banana-fisted I stared at her.

"Where is it?"

"Just up yon at the top of the hill, five minutes away, where your Daddy went to school."

"How would I get there from Grandma's?"

"Well, you'll have to stop with me in the week, and go out to the bungalow on Fridays after school. Would you like that?"

"Ooh, yes. When can I go?"

"On Monday. We've been to see the headmistress, and you can start next week. It's a pity to miss all your lessons, isn't it?"

So on Monday morning a slightly nervous new pupil turned up at the little Salcombe school on the hill. The children seemed to be all mixed up in one big room with fixed seats on a stepped floor. The girls were kind and friendly, as it was unusual to get a new girl from foreign parts. I was supplied with a pen, and a new exercise book, and did my best with the sums. The discipline was less strict than in my Newbury school, the atmosphere more relaxed, but there was no bad behaviour.

"Who's going to look after Peggy for me in the playground?" the teacher called out when it was break-time. Half a dozen hands shot up, but I took no notice. When we got into the playground I was surrounded by girls wanting to play with me, and all of them calling me Peggy. I shared my bag of grapes as far as they would go, and we then had a game of 'All in together this fine weather', with a long rope powerfully turned by two tall girls. When the bell went, and we walked in, (no lines), I said to Grace,

"My name's Jane, not Peggy."

"I'll tell her," Grace promised, and this she courageously did. But it was a day or two before I could repudiate Peggy.

We played skipping in all our playtimes. Each day I had fruit for my elevenses, given me from my kind Auntie Anne. This Tuesday it was a banana lying in my pocket waiting to be shared with Grace at a break in the game.

"Salt, mustard, vinegar, pepper
Salt, mustard, vinegar, pepper."

I slipped on something. Looking down I saw with deep regret a squashed banana. Grace was very sympathetic.

"No good now. 'E's all squashed. I'll put 'im in the bin for yer."

She picked it up and carried it, dangling despondently, to the dust-bin. What waste, I thought, as it flopped among the lunch bags.

At mid-day I ran home to Auntie Anne's for dinner, and told her about the sad end of the banana.

"Never mind about that, pet. Eat your dinner up. Grandpa's coming to fetch you this afternoon to get packed up. You're going back to Newbury tomorrow."

This was staggering! I could hardly believe it.

"What about school?"

"We can't help that. I know it's a pity when you've just settled in, but Daddy has sent for you. Peter is very ill."

I had many times visualised the day of my return. Daddy would write a letter -

"Mamma is better and has come home. Norma and Doreen are back from Tilehurst, and now you can come home. We shall all be together again."

It was not working out like that.

"Is Mamma home from the hospital?"

"No, but she is not in Reading now. She is in Abingdon. She won't be home just yet."

The whole thing happened in a flurry. There was no time to say goodbye to my new friends, to have a last look at the beach, or to go along the private lane to Uncle Arch's.

"Can I take my hoop, Grandma?"

"No, of course not. You'd look pretty silly with that on the train. You've got plenty of stuff back home for play."

We were off. No pleasant excitement at the prospect of a train journey. No joyous homecoming. Just an anxious, boring sit-down on the seat. Daddy met us with smiles and kisses, but something had happened to him. He had lost his buoyancy.

We settled to a routine at home. Grandma kept house whilst I went to school and Daddy went to work. I returned at once to my own school, to a teacher who did not know me. After the first lesson in the afternoon she said,

"All the scholarship girls can line up by the door."

"What does she mean?" I asked.

"Well, they're all the girls who are going in for the scholarship after Christmas."

I slipped out of my place.

"Please, Miss Hicks, I want to go in for the scholarship."

"Oh, well line up. I suppose it's all right."

We filed into the hall, where some old dual desks were set up at the end. There were girls from Standard Five as well. The headmistress was doing the coaching, sums first.

"Please, Miss Drew, I haven't learnt about cwts."

Irritation flashed out from her face and voice.

"Oh,. for goodness sake! As if it isn't hard enough! You go off holidaying for two months and come back expecting to sit for a scholarship! Four quarters one hundredweight, twenty hundredweights one ton. Now get on."

I got on. That was all the information I needed. In fact, it was the only hitch caused by my absence that I encountered. From then on I enjoyed the scholarship work.

Each day before going to work Daddy went to the hospital to see Peter. On Sundays he cycled the twenty miles each way to see Mamma in the sanatorium at Abingdon. There were several occasions when a friend of the family and his wife, a local jeweller, and later the Newbury archivist, took him to Abingdon in his car, and I was able to go as well to see my mother.

One evening, a few days after our return to Newbury, Grandma, Grandpa, Daddy and I went round to Craven Road to visit the other Grandma. It would be difficult to imagine two women more unlike than my two grandmas, but they talked quite pleasantly for the short while we were there. As we all walked home through the twilight, the adults were conversing sombrely in code, so I ran ahead and then back, and ahead again, like a dog.

"If you're in such a hurry, my dear, you can go on and unlock the door for us."

Daddy gave me the big key to the back door. I rushed on and opened it, and then, on an impulse of fun, (of which I was getting far too little), I hid behind the armchair. My father and his parents came in, and spoke a little, not knowing that I was in the room. All of a sudden I pricked up my ears.

"I suppose Jane doesn't know she's got a little brother?"

"No." It was a listless reply.

"Don't you think you ought to tell her, seeing as how he's out of danger?" More danger!

I came out. I had to sooner or later, and had no wish to be guilty of eavesdropping.

"Have we really got a new baby?"

"Yes, my dear. A little boy."

"What's his name?"

"He hasn't got a name yet. We'll think about it."

"Where is he?"

"He's still in hospital. He's not big enough or strong enough to come home yet. You'll see him soon."

"Is he with Mamma?"

"No, he's in Reading, and Mamma is in Abingdon, as you know."

My mind slid back to remember Doreen's arrival, the funny little holiday with Lucy at Craven Road, our homecoming, Mamma sitting up in the big bed with our new baby. What had gone wrong?

"That's three of our family in hospital then?"

"Time you got up that wooden hill, my girl." Thus Grandma. I ate my two petit beurre biscuits and went to clean my teeth, confused and unhappy.

About a week later Daddy mounted his bike as usual to visit Peter before setting off for work. I was ready for school and keen to go, as the house was not the cheerful place it had been. Standing by the window and looking out I was surprised to see Daddy riding back. He should have gone straight on to work. Propping his bike against the wall he came indoors and went at once to his mother.

"I've seen the last of my little boy." he said, and burst into tears.

She tried to console him, herself in tears, and the three of them totally forgot me. I was shattered to witness this adult grief in triplicate. It was school time, so I just took myself off.

The following days were trying and embarrassing ones. My friends, and many other children, continually tried to discuss Peter's death with me, and I steadily refused to admit them to our family's private concerns. I was constantly being told,

"Your little brother's dead, isn't he?" When I denied it they argued,

"Yes he is. My sister took a penny for his wreath."

Several of them, echoing parental conversation, informed me that it was a good job he had died, because otherwise he would have been funny in the head.

I was not aware of the funeral day in advance. Daddy just said,

"Will you go round to Mrs. Westgate's after school, Jane. She has kindly asked you to tea."

"All right." My voice was listless as his.

"Don't forget, will you? We shall all be out."

"I won't forget. I like going to tea with Mrs. Westgate."

We had a very nice tea, and the Westgates were even more kind than usual. They had a very small collection of books from which I was allowed to choose, among them 'Grimm's Fairy Tales'. The time passed very quickly as I read 'The Little Red Shoes', and 'Bluebeard', rapt with excitement and horror, but I little guessed what livid fears were fastening on my mind. It was time to go home, not a long walk, but a dark one, and I was a prey to the terrors of my imagination.

When I arrived safely my father and grandparents were there, sitting around doing nothing. The men were both wearing their Sunday suits, with black ties. Grandma had on a black dress which I had never seen before, and on the shelf was a rolled-up pair of black gloves. The funeral was over.

"We're going home on Friday, Jane. Are you going to stay and keep your Daddy company?"

"Yes."

"That's a good girl. Do all you can to help him, won't you? He's got enough trouble on his hands."

"Yes."

It was eight o'clock. I took my loneliness and sorrow, and lack of hope along with the dreadful Little Red Shoes and Bluebeard, up to bed.

Peter was buried on a bright October day, with leaves falling softly from the trees.

CHAPTER EIGHTEEN

By Friday afternoon Daddy and I were the sole occupants of the house. The days which followed were strange ones. We lived on endless pork and beans, corned beef, fried apples, bread and cheese, cocoa. Each day when school was over I went to tea with one or other of my friends, or with Grandma in Craven Road, or with the Westgates. At five past five Daddy got home from work, and I returned to the house, unless a friend had especially requested me to stay for the evening. There was a little homework to be done, because of the coming scholarship examination, and then it was time for bed.

Lucy came home from school for Christmas, her third end-of-term, and things brightened considerably. We were alone all day in the house, as of course it was my school holiday as well, and we had a good deal of fun, tempered by a continued sense of guilt because we had not done the washing-up. Daddy did not expect us to keep the house spick and span, but it was not unreasonable to ask us to wash up the dishes and put them away whilst he was at work. It was not that Lucy and I intended to skive; we just procrastinated, and occasionally Daddy would arrive home to find the job not done.

"Do you want a piece of cake?" Lucy asked one morning, casually, as if she were the mother.

I opened startled eyes. I did of course, but would never have dared.

Lucy went into the larder and brought out the cake tin, setting it down on the rug by the fire where we had been playing. She fetched a knife and cut off two large slices of the lemon-rice cake which Daddy had bought at the 'International Stores'. She then got two old copies of 'The Amateur Photographer' to put them on, (it would have been silly to have increased the already big pile of washing-up), and we ate them with mixed feelings of pleasure and guilt.

"Do you think Daddy will notice?" I asked.

"What if he does? We've got to be fed. It'll be ages till dinner, and that won't be much for two growing girls."

Lucy was certainly developing at Christ's Hospital!

To relieve our consciences we did all the washing-up after this dubious deed. If Daddy noticed the diminishing cake he did not mention it. We went through all the normal Christmas routines and rites; we hung up paper chains, bought a six-penny Christmas tree from Woolworth's, and climbed on the dresser to reach the box of baubles which Mamma always used to produce just at Christmas time. Never before had we thought of touching that box ourselves, but times had changed.

"You won't be hanging up stockings this year, will you?" Daddy asked hopefully.

"Of course we shall. We always do. Can we take one of your socks?"

"Well, don't expect much to happen if you do."

"Why not? Father Christmas isn't in trouble, is he?"

"You'd be surprised!"

The trouble was that Daddy was in a cleft stick. Having brought us up to believe in Santa Claus with a whole-hearted enthusiasm, he was now hard put to it to come up to expectations. Also he was in some doubt as to the age children reach before the legend was inevitably exploded. Common sense had told us the truth, but we were hanging on to a happy myth.

So we took our socks up to bed. It seemed dull and flat without Mamma and the little ones, but we got out of it all we could. We chatted companionably in our double bed and did not notice how late it was getting. The living-room door opened and Daddy called up,

"Go to sleep, you two. I'm not going to wait all night."

Santa Claus was dead!

It was a strange, hollow Christmas, although the toys were the most expensive we had ever had. I had a really big doll, baby-shaped, which was what I wanted. I called her Christina, because we had recently had to learn -

"Does the road wind uphill all the way?
Yes, to the very end."

It was a sad afternoon when Lucy and I decided to give the new Christina a bath. Daddy was at work and we were whiling away the time in the house. We put hot water in the little galvanised tub and sat Christina in it. All was well for a few minutes, and Christina loved it. Then we noticed that her legs were going soft and whipped her out immediately. Too late! From that day Christina was condemned to a one-legged existence, and I had only had her a week! This would not have happened if we had had someone at home who could have foreseen such a result.

The holiday came to an end, and Lucy's tearful departure was over once again. It was back to school for me too, and almost time for the scholarship examinations. But another change was imminent. Baby Patrick came home from hospital.

It was Grandma who cared for him. There was no-one else. I went round to Craven Road at the first opportunity to see him. He was a pretty baby, with dark blue eyes and a serious expression, very ready to smile at everyone. Grandma still had his body wrapped in oil-soaked cotton-wool, whether by hospital orders or by her own old-fashioned ideas I did not know. He took his bottle of milk from me without demur, and soon became fond of me because I saw him frequently, and was able to help Grandma by feeding him.

It was hard for her to have to rear this delicate baby. She had brought up eight of her own, and seen them off her hands, and here she was, tending Patrick, 'a light sleeper, and a little under weight'.

He was a seven months baby, and had made a poor start. Grandma very soon became tired, and often complained of her lot. She certainly deserved sympathy, but it was Patrick I was more sorry for.

January passed, and in February I sat for my two examinations. The Christ's Hospital examination was held in the Council Chambers, in a dark, lofty room totally unsuitable for the purpose. This examination included dictation, and one needed to concentrate to follow the gruff voice of the elderly man conducting the test, as it rumbled huskily among the dark old rafters high up above the dust-dotted shafts of winter sun. There would be no results until May, so we forgot all about the examinations once they were over. I felt confident of having done quite well, although there was only one vacancy for Christ's Hospital that year.

My daily visit to help Grandma was becoming something of a chore. Much as I loved little Patrick I sometimes felt that it would have been nice to go on home and play marbles with the other girls. I hinted as much one day.

"Oh no! You will come here as usual. I'm not young enough for all this work, and it's your duty to help me. After all, he is your little brother."

For a few moments my sense of logic was at war with my sense of justice. Grandma's burden, though heavy, was hardly of my making. And what I had long thought of as a voluntary act of kindness on my part was apparently an inescapable and expected duty. Trapped, was how I felt.

"And in the holiday." Grandma continued, "You'll have more time free, so I shall expect you round here every morning till dinner-time."

My heart sank.

"But Lucy will be home in the holidays, and she'll have no-one to play with."

"I can't help that. You'll have plenty of time to play with her in the afternoons."

When Lucy arrived home for Easter I told her of my bondage.

"Well," she declared, "if you're round there working every day you won't have any holiday, so you can't go round in your holidays."

Good thinking! But I could not see it appealing to Grandma.

For several days I trotted round at half past nine to dust and sweep and wash-up, and to give Patrick his feed. One morning I had an idea.

"Do you think Lucy and I could take Patrick for a walk?"

"Yes, I suppose so. That would be nice for Lucy."

For the rest of the holiday we pushed the pram out each morning, and enjoyed it. Patrick was by then six months old and a responsive baby, and a bond of affection sprang up between the three of us.

Early in the summer term the results of the first stage of the examinations were received. I had passed in both and had two interviews to attend in June. But the more immediately interesting event was the arrival of Auntie Edith to look after us and keep house, which meant that Patrick could at last come home.

Auntie Edith was a state registered nurse and a hospital sister. It was a great sacrifice for her to give up her job for over a year to care for her sister's five children. She never married, but seemed to handle children with a natural ease, and coped kindly and efficiently with a difficult situation.

I was by now in Standard Six and enjoying a more satisfying curriculum. We had an elderly class teacher who really liked and understood the girls she taught. Our literary experience was extended to include authentic, (although shortened), classics, 'David Copperfield', 'The Old Curiosity Shop', 'Tom Sawyer'. She took trouble to explain any unknown words to us, and broadened our outlook by talking of her own experiences.

It was Auntie Edith who made me clean and tidy for my interviews, and told me how to behave. The High School oral was held in the headmistress's study. We sat on a very polished bench in the entrance hall until the stiffly-starched maid asked us to go in. There were about nine of us, and we were all interviewed together. Each of us read aloud in turn, and the headmistress asked us questions on the text. Then she tested us on mental arithmetic, and turned us out.

The Christ's Hospital interview was quite different. There were only three girls who had scored highly enough for interview, and we were asked to attend at the Council Chamber at nine o'clock one Friday morning. We sat by a big, heavy, shiny table whilst an elderly man asked us questions. Some were to be answered orally, some on paper.

He started by asking each of us what we had had for breakfast.

"Bacon and egg," the first girl told him.

"And where do you think the bacon came from?" etc. etc.

My breakfast had been Shredded Wheat.

"Where do you think the wheat was grown?"

We were there about an hour, and when dismissed went straight on to school.

Auntie Edith took an interest in me because I was the only one at home old enough to talk to. Walking down to the town one day she drew my attention to the election posters displayed everywhere.

"When you are old enough to vote which party will you vote for?"

"I don't know. I don't understand about it."

"You ought to know the basic principles of politics. There are three parties in Parliament, Conservatives, Liberals and Labour. Conservatives like to keep all the old things going; the Labour party wants to help the ordinary working people, and the Liberals are something in between."

"Well, then I think I shall vote for Labour."

"Yes, I think I shall."

Simplistic as it was, this gave me my very earliest insight into party politics.

Once Lucy was back at school more strange things seemed to be afoot. Auntie Edith suddenly began to get a great many letters, all in different handwritings, which she opened eagerly at the breakfast table, and replaced in their envelopes at once. I wondered, but said nothing. Then one morning baby Patrick upset his mug of milk all over the tablecloth, and over himself.

"Oh dear," Auntie said, lifting the dripping baby out of his high chair.

"Get the cloth, Jane, will you?"

Off I went and came back with a dishcloth, and mopped up the mess while Auntie dried the baby. Propped against the tea-cosy was one of those letters, open before my very eyes. I could not help seeing it.

"Sorry I cannot accept situation as housekeeper. Too many children etc."

So that was it. Auntie was tired of us, and wanted to go and be a nurse again. I was not surprised, but it hurt. I said nothing, and for some days nothing happened. Then -

"A lady is coming to see you this afternoon. I want you to be very good, all of you, and show her what nice children you can be."

"What is her name?"

"Miss Laycock. If she likes you she might be coming to live here and look after you all. Wouldn't that be nice?"

(I doubt it. I really do doubt it. I wish Auntie could stay till Mamma comes home. I wish Mamma would come home.)

The lady arrived in time for tea. She was not our idea of a lady. Her speech was broad, broader even than mine. She said 'Ta' for thankyou, and 'Don't you want no more?' It was an embarrassing, tense meal. We did not feel naturally drawn towards her.

"Is she coming to live here, Auntie?"

"Yes, I think so. We shall know in a day or two."

She came, and she stayed. We grew fond of her by default, because she was running our home and, in her way, caring for us. She evidently hoped that we would return her love, which was impossible. The younger children adapted more easily than Lucy and I, but as Lucy was away at school most of the time the battles and heartaches, the tempers, and hatred, and emotional reconciliations were my lot.

A strange anomaly now arose. Mamma was coming home. It was not the home-coming I had so yearned for. She was 'Not quite well yet', and would have to rest in bed a lot, and for this reason Miss Laycock would not be leaving us. But the mere presence of my mother in the house, to be deferred to at any time, was a joy and a comfort. I spent many hours in her bedroom, and we talked of everything that came into our heads. She told me a great deal about the Royal Family, about the two little princesses, Elizabeth and Margaret Rose, about astronomy, astrology, about the colours of jewels and their values, about her own schooldays, her parents, her father's business failure.

The results of the scholarship examinations came out in due course. I had passed for the High School, but the Christ's Hospital place had been awarded to the oldest of the three girls. This was a sensible decision officially, as I could have taken the examination again the following year, but I did not know, and my parents did not realise this. I was bitterly disappointed, and felt that I had failed, but as the summer wore on I began to look forward to going to the High School.

Miss Laycock did the necessary shopping for items of uniform, and my mother made my school tunic and white blouses. I can recall her struggles with the intractible, fraying navy-blue serge, her near despair with the three box pleats front and back, but she managed it. As I was less than four feet in height I was entitled to wear black socks instead of stockings, and would have preferred to, but Mamma thought it best for me to go into stockings from the start, most likely fearing that I would have reached the mandatory height limit before the socks were worn out. So I had a liberty bodice with four suspenders, a navy tunic, white blouse, navy-blue knickers and black shoes and stockings. We wore cloth hats like small sou' westers with the school badge on the front. My great pride and joy was the purple tie, very silky. I felt I had arrived.

CHAPTER NINETEEN

It was an early autumn day when I first walked along the Enborne Road in the glory of my new school uniform, wearing a satchel containing nothing. Where now stand the houses called 'Enborne Rise' there was then a low-lying field, and on this day it was mysterious with thin, drifting patches of morning mist. We turned to the left by Robinson's Bakery, past the boys' Grammar School on our right, along Buckingham Road with its free-growing lime trees, now severely pollarded, and into school. Not through the front entrance with its great, imposing gates as we had done on interview, but through the wooden side gate in Andover Road.

Once seated at our desks, our first task was to fill in our timetable as dictated by the form-mistress. It sounded exciting. There were new subjects in it, science, geometry, algebra, French, gymnastics. Out in my shoe-bag was a new pair of plimsolls with lovely crepe soles, just waiting to be used, and also my science overall of butcher-blue cotton, made by Mamma from the pattern provided.

This done our form-mistress called the register, to find out who was who, and said,

"Are there any girls here who are still ten?"

I put up my hand, and look round surreptitiously. There was one other, a small, pale, mousy girl called Gina. We were to spend seven years getting to know each other.

Our first lessons in science dealt with crystal formation, dissolving, and saturated solutions. Having helped Daddy many times to make saturated solutions of hyposulphite of soda for photographic purposes I was quite at home with this. His method had been to put the exact quantity of chemicals into a lemonade bottle with the right amount of water and get one of the children to shake like beano until it had all dissolved. At school we had a beaker, and stirred it scientifically with a little glass stick. We then moved on to the business of heat and expansion, new to me, and fascinating.

English lessons took a big leap from what we had been doing at the Council School. Our literature for the first term consisted of the usual novel, poetry, and drama, 'The Christmas Carol', 'Ballads and Ballad-poems', and 'Julius Caesar'. The ballads were fresh to me, except for 'Barbara Allen', which we had known as a song. I have never totally overcome the sense of sheer horror which dropped around me as we read 'Edward' for the first time. 'Julius Caesar' frightened me too. It was not a deep, psychological fear, just a surface fear of the cloak-and-dagger conspiracy, and all that blood. I was a bit surprised at the High School going in for that sort of thing.

Our friend Laura had been a year at the High School when I started there. She was Lucy's age, so I do not know how it was that we came to be in the same form, but we were, and it was fun, although perhaps unfortunate in that we were both mischievous children. We played up the weaker members of staff, and egged each other on to unruly behaviour, which led to our being separated. I found myself in Upper Three B, and Laura was in Upper Three A. This sobered me a little, and for a while. Most of our teachers were well in control of their classes, and at such lessons I made no attempt to cause a disturbance. But where a teacher was weak, and incapable of stimulating enough interest in her subject I could not resist the temptation to play the fool and make the other girls laugh.

My favourite lesson in that first year was gymnastics, which came twice a week on the timetable, following French. We were allowed to sit through our French lessons on Tuesdays and Fridays wearing our plimsolls to save time. Un - deux - trois -, and a smashing smell of rubber. When the bell went we lined up by the door quivering with excitement, until Miss Barry said,

"En avant, mes enfants," and off we scampered to the annexe, and joy among the ropes and bars.

At the end of the first term all the new girls had a medical. Once again the heart murmur was noticed, but this time it did me no good, as for the rest of my schooldays I had no gymnastics or games. This was deprivation indeed! I did not so much mind missing field games, as I did find it a strain to rush up and down the pitch for any length of time, but I loved apparatus work in the gymnasium. Had I been allowed to go into the library and read I would have resented it less, but I was always told to go out and watch, and to do some lifeless practice with a lacrosse stick, with no end in view at all. In the gymnasium too, I was given useful little things to do, like holding the end of a rope, putting a foot on the base of the jumping stand to steady it, (the stand at the other end was steady enough without me), or getting out the coloured braids. It was a waste of time.

My friendship with Laura had deepened during those first few High School years. Living near to each other meant that we could continue our common interests out of school hours, so we borrowed each other's books and shared our sweets. For one year only we could help each other with homework.

Laura's Mum was a generous, permissive parent. Her home was always open to the friends of her children. I liked going into their house, because not only was it fun to be with this easy-going family, but because the house itself was an exact replica of ours, only the other way round. Their rooms, and stairs, and fireplaces, bathroom and kitchen sink were identical with ours, but on opposite sides, and I was always astounded at the total difference between two homes built from the same pattern.

Whenever Lucy came home for holidays we played together with Laura and Jeanie as of old, and it was with the four of us that the I. C. was first set up.

The initials stood for 'Ideas Club'. Lucy and I had decided to make some stilts one day, and we went into the shed where lengths of wood were stacked against the wall. Having selected two of equal and suitable size we picked up two small, thick blocks and nailed them on about nine inches from the bottom. Hammers and nails and sandpaper were always available. The result was good and we took turns in practising stilt-walking round the garden. Unfortunately, as every carpenter knows, two nails are not enough to support the full weight of a half-grown girl, and the steps kept falling off. We tried string as a supplement to the nails, but still the steps fell off. We put our problem to Daddy when he came home, and he took out the nails and replaced them with screws.

"But even that won't last long," he told us. "You need a different design altogether."

Before long we had a really good pair of stilts, designed and made by our father, and we became very proficient with them. When we appeared on the green and in the road walking confidently on our stilts we created quite a sensation. Everyone wanted to try them, but on-one else could use them properly. We were convinced that we had invented them.

"We ought to invent some more things," Lucy said. "We might be famous."

"Yes, we could invent some more toys. Anyway, we've already invented long hair for dressing-up. That's one more thing."

The 'long-hair' was a favourite game of ours whenever we could get hold of some tow-rope, much favoured at that time for tying up large parcels. It had to be shared equally between us, then we proceeded to cut up our portion into lengths of about a foot. These we tied to a circle of elastic which fitted the head. The rope could then be untwisted and teased out with the fingers, brushed, combed and arranged over our own hair, which was short and almost straight. It was a wonderful ash-blonde colour, and could be curled and waved by merely pressing into shape. Whole rows of ringlets could be produced by winding round a finger. We were transformed at once into fairies, princesses, posh ladies and lucky schoolgirls with long hair, and the wigs thus created survived brushing, combing and curling for many days.

"Obviously," Lucy added, when reminded of this, "We are inventors, and we could start a society."

"Laura and Jeanie can belong, can't they?"

"Of course, and many, many more children, as long as they invent things."

"Yes." I was working up a tremendous enthusiasm. "But don't let's let them join unless they can invent things."

"We shall have to call it something." Lucy liked her ends neatly tied. "What about 'The Inventors' New Natural Society'?"

"That's a silly name. It will only be new at first, and there's no point in calling it 'natural'. It sounds stupid!"

"Well," Lucy insisted, "I thought if we called it that we could make it 'Inns' for short."

One of the first effects of boarding school on Lucy was her craze to reduce everything to initials. Christ's Hospital was inevitably C. H. The odd box in which we kept pencils and bits of crayon became the G. P. B., or in full, the General Pencil Box.

"It's stupid. Nobody will want to join it. Let's just call it the 'Club'."

"All right then," Lucy amended, "The Inventors' Club'." We rushed off to find Laura and Jeanie.

As anticipated, they were highly enthusiastic. We agreed to tell a few of our other friends and to meet in Laura's garden that evening. Her garden was a delight to me after our flowerless stretch of grass. Pansies grew there, and love-in-the-mist, and a strange shrub which they called 'Boys' Love', the smell of which attracted and repelled me at the same time.

Our first meeting was much enjoyed, although little was actually invented. It was, perhaps, more of a business meeting, with officers electing themselves on the strength of its having been their idea in the first place. We decided to meet once a week, taking turns to host the members in our gardens. We would each pay a half-penny a time for funds, (although it was not clear what needed funding), and each member was expected to invent something each week and bring it to the meeting. No-one ever declared this meeting closed, as there was quite a lot of A. O. B., such as playing French cricket and getting drinks of water from Laura's Mum's kitchen. It was a most satisfactory inception.

"Mamma, we've got a new club. It's the 'I. C.' We've had a meeting in Laura's, and there are eight members already."

"Sounds interesting. What do you do?"

Mamma was ironing. I watched her passing the iron over the huge white sheet, back and forth, back and forth, her face flushed with the warm work on a warm evening. The smell of steam from the air-dried linen was delicious.

"We invent things. We're called the 'Inventors' Club'."

"And what have you invented?"

"Well, it began with Lucy and me. We invented stilts, and long hair, you know, out of rope, but we've all got to invent something every week."

"Mm."

Mamma went outside to the scullery and changed the iron for a hotter one, leaving the first on the smallest gas jet turned low. She returned, holding the iron close to her cheek to assess its temperature, and continued to transform the sheet.

"You know, you didn't really invent stilts. You made some, but people have been using stilts for hundreds of years. Inventing something means making something which has never yet been thought of."

"I know, but we didn't know what to call it. It was our idea to make some first out of all our friends."

"Well, why not call it the 'Ideas Club'? It will still be the 'I. C.'."

A little unwillingly we agreed to drop the pretentious title, and at the next meeting the members were informed that we had changed the name. It was now the 'Ideas Club'. Did I imagine a shadow of relief on a few faces?

For this second meeting Lucy and I shared an 'idea'; and showed everyone how to make a rush basket. Jeanie told us how to make a straw hat for a doll, but gave no demonstration. Laura had been practising tunes on grasses stretched between her fingers, in which I knew her to be an expert, although her performance that evening left much to be desired. Daphne showed us how to do a cat's cradle, the old, boring, common one we had all been doing for years, and we did not hesitate to tell her. A few of the members had had no time, etc. etc.

At Laura's the previous week we had had an informal grouping of the club, but I was ambitious for something a little more highly organised, so I told them all to sit on the bottom strand of the wire fence. This kept them all basically lined-up. I had also had another brilliant idea. One of our members, called Ida, was an only child with a wonderful supply of toys, and also of books, notably some very big, exciting annuals.

"Why don't we have a club library?" I suggested.

This was not my 'idea for the week', but just a gratis offering.

"If we all brought one or two books each we could all borrow them, and I'll write down who's got them."

The proposal was carried by a unanimous shout of votes. I then, in passing, mentioned that it would be quite alright for the library to be kept in our house, as I had a box. This was agreed. We still have a copy of 'Alice in Wonderland' with 'I. C.' written inside in red crayon.

With the return of school and the onset of autumn and winter the 'I. C.' went into hibernation. But it did not die. The seed had been sown, dropped, and lay dormant, only awaiting a more clement season to raise its busy little head again.

CHAPTER TWENTY

It was Brenda, (whose garden ran down to the canal), who first set me thinking about joining the Girl Guides. She told me casually one day at Sunday School that she was going to Guides the next evening.

"You lucky thing!" I screeched. "I wish I could join."

Laura was a Guide, and I had already asked if I could join, but Mamma and Daddy were agreed that most of the girls parading about in uniform were not the best-behaved girls in Newbury.

"Ask your Mamma again. Tell her I'm going to join."

I did ask, in vain, but Brenda's mother did me a good turn. She came round a few evenings later, with Brenda, to discuss it with my father.

"I was just of your opinion, you know, until a few weeks ago. But recently I have heard a lot of good things about the Guides, especially the company that meets in the Drill Hall on Mondays. Brenda enjoys it very much and it doesn't seem to make her rowdy."

Daddy had been playing his violin when they arrived. He stood by the music stand, still with the instrument tucked under his chin and keen to get back to his practising. He was unconvinced, but under a three-fold female attack.

"My husband and I," Brenda's Mamma continued, "Always thought the Girl Guides were the riff-raff of the town, but . . ."

"That's it exactly," Daddy interrupted her, laying his violin resignedly but reverently, in its blue satin nest. "That's just what I think, the riff-raff of the town."

"But they're not that really, I have been to one of their meetings. It was most orderly, and the Captain is a real lady."

Daddy sat exercising his fingers with great concentration. I said nothing, knowing that his resistance was weakening, but deeming it wiser to wait on time.

"I'll tell my wife what you have said. She's in bed now. And if she thinks there's no harm in it, and as Brenda's joined, I won't stand in the way of Jane."

And so, to my immediate delight, and lasting benefit, I became a Girl Guide. Ours was an excellent company, taking its strength and success from our Captain, Miss Marjorie Holder. I liked and trusted her from the very start of our long acquaintance.

Since I was a friend of Laura, who was a Robin, I was a Robin too. But I soon took a liking to a dark-eyed, lively girl in the Kingfisher patrol, whose name was Meg. At first the only bond between Meg and myself was our wild enthusiasm for Guiding. Both of us, and Laura too, lived from Monday to Monday. After the meetings Meg often wandered round into the avenue with Laura and me. She eventually joined my Sunday School, and a life-long friendship had begun.

Enthusiasm seemed to be the criterion for promotion within the Guide Company. When a vacancy arose for a Canary patrol second I was chosen, rather to my surprise, so I died as a Robin and metamorphosed as a Canary. The Canary patrol was a poor and rather despised lot, never winning any games or gaining any badges. Before long I was again promoted, from Second to Patrol leader of the Canaries, and then we began to give the Robins and the Kingfishers a run for their money.

The annual camp came up for discussion early in June. We were seated in a circle on the floor enjoying our camp-fire sing-song, and expecting another instalment of Ratty and Moley, but to our disappointment Captain said she was going to talk to us, and we were to listen very carefully.

The camp was being held this year at Beenham, a Berkshire village about eight miles distant. Laura looked at me and made a face of disappointment.

"They went to the sea last year. I wish we could go to the sea."

Captain explained that a seaside camp was much more expensive, and in order to keep costs down we alternated our choice of sites between sea and country from year to year. The cost of the camp this year would be one pound, for ten days' full board and lodging with fare included. My heart sank. I dared not ask for a pound.

At the end of the meeting Captain caught me just as we were setting off for home.

"Is your mother still in bed, Jane?"

"Yes, but she's a bit better." (Always the self-persuasion born of hope.)

"I would like to come and see her. Do you think she would mind?"

"Ooh, no. She wouldn't mind. She'd like you to come."

"Wednesday morning then. You've got time to let me know if that is inconvenient.

I was at school of course when she came to visit, and I have no idea of what was discussed, but Mamma said when I went up to see her at dinner time,

"You're Guide Captain really is a very nice lady, Jane. We had a long talk. She wants to take you to camp in the holidays. Would you like to go?"

I was almost in tears with joy. It was so unexpected.

"Don't you want to go?"

"Yes. I was dying to go, but I didn't think it was much use asking."

"If Daddy agrees that will be all right, and I think I can persuade him."

And so I proudly put my name on the camping list at the next meeting, and prepared for a whole month's wait.

"I suppose it will be nothing but kit, kit, kit for the next three weeks now." Mamma said, not irritably, but with amusement. A kit-bag was borrowed from somewhere, and grey blankets from somewhere else. (Those were not the days of luxurious, zip-up sleeping-bags.) Mamma made my camp overall, a simple enough task for one who had wrestled with a serge gym tunic, and also the camp hat, a protection against the very hot sun. I put them all on and ran up the road to show Laura.

"Ooh, you look nice! Mum hasn't made mine yet. Come in and show her what they're supposed to look like."

We went in, and Laura's Mum cast a professional eye over my outfit. She was a dressmaker.

"Your Mamma's good with her machine, you know. She's done them beautifully. I must get on with Laura's. I was going to offer to make yours for you, but you've beaten me to it."

I cannot remember what were the results of the end-of-term examinations. I am certain that neither of us gave due attention to our homework and revision. We could think of nothing but getting ready for camp.

We travelled on a private local bus which picked us up at Green and Whincup's garage in West Street. A lorry was there as well, and onto this went the tents, pots and pans, stores, and all our kit-bags. We climbed aboard the bone-shaker of a bus and at last were off.

When we arrived all our kit and equipment was dumped in piles in the field, and there we were. Panic seized me.

"We can't stay here for ten days!" I thought. There was simply no sign of any amenity.

We were allotted a helper to each group, and staggered off in fours with the heavy tent we had been given to erect. Laura and I were together, with two girls we did not know very well. We pegged and hammered and pulled, until the tent was ready to be raised.

"You can crawl in, Jane. You're the smallest."

Conscious that the cheerful spirit of Guiding was being strongly assailed by a sick desire to go home, I took the pole and scrambled under the thick, hot canvas. With some difficulty I managed to keep the head of the pole in the socket and pushed. Aided by the outside pushers up went the canvas, and at once I experienced another novel sensation. Where, a moment before, had been a stretch of flaccid canvas lying on the grass, now suddenly there was shelter and living space. A home has arisen! It was a primitive, instinctive thrill. My doubt and depression vanished in that instant, and a deep satisfaction filled my whole being.

All around the field bell-tents were springing up like mushrooms. When all were safely pitched according to our Captain's high standards we went round visiting and first-footing. The cook-house whistle reminded us all that we were hungry, so we sat on groundsheets and partook of thick sandwiches made from new bread and butter and potted meat from a big earthenware dish. Mugs of tea and apples completed our first camp meal, and we were then sent off to furnish our tents.

Everyone had brought a pillowcase from home, and Captain handed each of us a palliasse, like an empty mattress cover. These we carried across the field and into the barn, where we filled them both with straw.

"Not too full," Captain warned us, "Or you'll bounce off."

Inside the tent the straw mattresses were laid upon groundsheets, and the blankets, folded into each other to give as much warmth below as above, were placed on top.

"I shall never sleep on that pillow," Laura declared. "I'm used to two feather ones at home." I was not sure.

We had practised at our Guide meetings making little gadgets and fitments for use in the tent; sticks lashed to the tent pole were pegs for clothes, two notched twigs lashed to lengths of wood kept our shoes off the ground. Kit-bags had to be raised on stick platforms to keep them free from damp. We were all busy and happy, thrilled with this back-to-nature holiday.

A long latrine trench had been dug before we arrived, and surrounded by a hessian screen. It was sectioned off into four, and each latrine was equipped with a box seat with a hole in the top. In each compartment a shovel lay on the heap of loose soil which had been dug out and piled at the back. The 'door' could be tied with tape for privacy, if one was not in a hurry, and the wind blew freely in and out and round about. The end latrine was labelled 'Guiders Only'. These were our sanitary arrangements.

The health patrol for the day was expected to inspect the guy ropes supporting the hessian screen, to loosen or tighten them according to the weather outlook, to go round the pegs with the mallet, to check supplies of toilet roll in each compartment, and to wield a supplementary shovel where shovelling had been inadequate. We got used to even this quite quickly. Everything was fun.

The rising whistle sounded at seven-thirty, and cook-house at eight-thirty, when we assembled on the groundsheets laid out by the orderlies. Each Guide brought her own two enamel plates, mug, and eating tools to the meal, and washed them at the end.

The next hour was spent on patrol work, quite a lot of it, and then we had a short free time. When we were at the sea this was the time for going to the beach, and in the water. Camp dinner was the big meal of the day, and clearing it up was an onerous job. Then followed compulsory rest, on our palliasses brought outside if fine. We looked forward to this, as it was preceded by tuck-shop, where we could spend our pennies on sweets and fruit, and take them with us to eat while we lay down to rest and read.

The camp fire hour was the climax of the whole busy day. In the cool of the evening with daylight fading owls hooted, crickets sang and glowworms occasionally glowed. We sang till our voices were tired, and then Captain read to us from 'Tales of the Great Outdoors', bringing the characters to life in a quite remarkable way. We stood round the dying fire to sing 'Taps', (why so named no-one was able to tell me). It had the sound of a bugle call.

'Day is done, gone the sun
From the sea, from the hills, from the sky.
All is well, safely rest.
God is nigh.'

"Off you go now. Get to bed as quickly as you can. Goodnight."

Goodnights rang out all round the field. By nine o'clock everything was peaceful. We could occasionally see the flash of torches through the canvas as the adults moved quietly about to see that all was well.

Besides Laura and me our tent housed Thelma and Kathleen. Kathleen had a brand new toothbrush to bring to camp. Ours were used ones.

"I don't expect she's ever had one before," Laura said, "That's why."

Kathleen's toothbrush stayed nice and new till she went home. Her Lifebuoy soap stayed new too.

"Are you awake, Jane?" That was Laura's voice.

"Yes."

"I'm cold. Are you?"

"A bit."

"Put your bed up near mine. We'll be warmer."

This we proceeded to do, until I had a better idea.

"Let's undo all the blankets and make a double bed." We were both used to sharing with a sister.

We set to work, with much whispering and giggling. A light flashed on the canvas wall and Captain's head appeared in the doorway.

"You should be asleep. What are you up to?"

"We're making a double bed, Captain."

"Right. Only do it quietly. You're keeping others awake."

We all learned to sleep deeply on the prickly, noisy straw, surrounded by the smell of cows and of aromatic, dewy soil.

Not all the Guides enjoyed camp. Quite a number of them came once only, being unable to adapt to the life of hard work, co-operation, lack of comforts and the inescapable proximity of nature.

CHAPTER TWENTY-ONE

While these years were slipping by Newbury itself was undergoing changes. One change I deeply regretted was the stripping of the Virginia Creeper from the walls of the Methodist Church. Set there by someone who liked to see a splash of colour against the grey stone, this one small climbing plant had spread over the whole surface of the building. Picturesque in spring in its dress of shiny green leaves, it was by autumn a fiery landmark of scarlet and crimson.

The trustees decided, and rightly, that the creeper was eating into the masonry, and men of the church set to work to remove it. For a while I felt sensitive about its nakedness.

Great changes were taking place in the shopping area as well. Opposite the Post Office, where is now a photographic processing shop stood a useful shop called the Red Stores, appropriately painted. The ground floor was not large, but there was an upstairs, which gave it status as well as space. It was a popular shop because whilst mothers were in there buying vests and liberty bodices, saucepans and tea-towels, the children could look at the toys. Father Christmas often shopped there, I think, judging by what many children got in their stockings.

In about 1927 the Red Stores must have been disturbed to hear that Newbury was to have an even redder store. Woolworth's had a foot in the commercial doorway.

The residents were excited and proud when they heard about it, because until then Woolworth's had been to them one of the wonders of the bigger towns. Now they were to take over Penford's Store, next to Camp Hopson's in Northbrook Street. There was a good deal of publicity about the opening. A cash prize was offered to the first customer who would spend a pound. The 'Newbury News' carried big notices of the date of opening, and of the bargains which would be available. Woolworth's went to the expense of printing cards advertising the opening, with little gramophone records stuck on to the middle. Every household had one dropped through the door. I claimed ours as my own, and took great care of it. We had no gramophone.

"Who can play it, Daddy?"

"I don't know. It won't be much good anyway."

"But it will play, won't it?"

"I suppose so. You'd best ask Mrs. Westgate. They've got a gramophone."

He did not mean it seriously, and I knew he did not, but I was determined to hear my own record played, so I called in at Mrs. Westgate's after school the next day and asked her if she would put it on for me. I expect she was very busy, and not in the mood to listen to little records with the next day's milk round to get ready, but she showed no impatience. She turned out a drawer to find the handle, opened the machine and put the small card on the turntable. The needle had to be changed, of course, one needle one record in those days, and the gramophone had to be fully wound up. At last she pushed the starter and playback began. It had one great merit. It was short. The first few grooves gave the date of Woolworth's opening and a list of the bargains unprecedented, and this was followed by a brief jingle whose every line ended with -

'And there's nothing over sixpence in the stores.'

It had a thin, wobbling melody line, because the card was riding up and down under the weight of the arm, but I was satisfied. My record 'went'. I carried it back home with pride, although that was the first and last time it was played.

Our Christmas shopping loyalty was now transferred to Woolworth's. It was a small, single-hall shop at first, just one third of its present width and half the length, and it was always packed to suffocation on Saturdays and at the run-up to Christmas.

Newbury had two cinemas at this time, as far as I can remember. There was the 'Picture Palace', next to the Methodist Church, where there are now two shops. This was an ancient and primitive building with hard seats, where I once went with Laura on a Saturday morning to see Jackie Coogan. It was my first experience of 'pictures' and I could have stayed there, cold as I was, all day. This 'Picture Palace' was closed when I was very small. The other cinema was the 'Carlton', built, I believe by a member of the Tufnail family. This was almost opposite the Post Office and near the Red Stores, and came to be referred to as the 'flea-pit'. It had red plush tip-up seats, and was a comfortable little place by the standards of the time, in spite of its unfair reputation for being dirty. I visited the Carlton only once. It survived the Second World War, but was soon afterwards destroyed by fire.

Newbury was by the mid 1920's a fast-growing town, and it was in about 1927 that my father started a new job. They were to build a new cinema in Bartholomew Street, and he was taken on as a carpenter and joiner. We were naturally very proud to see this large new building taking shape and to know that he was having a hand in its erection. At last the shell was completed, and then began a long wait for opening day.

When the 'Regal' was finished there was a delightful surprise in store for me. Each employee was given two free tickets for the opening show, and this meant that Daddy and I could go. We went to the matinee in the afternoon. As we walked up the shallow, cathedral-like steps I was quite overawed by the grandeur, the newness, the amount of gilt paint and the wonder of its dimming lights. Pride was upper-most, that Newbury should have such a place of entertainment, and that my father had helped to make it.

We saw the 'Pathe Gazette' news, a short cartoon of Donald Duck, and then the main feature, called 'Canaries Sometimes Sing'. It was a gangster film, almost too exciting to bear. I waited all through to see the canaries, but none appeared, to my disappointment. Daddy did not seem to think much of the show, which astounded me. I found it the last word in comfort, luxury and excitement. It is not to be wondered at that I watched with regret the demolition of the 'Regal'.

When I was about nine I took to going for little walks on my own, and no-one seemed to mind. Usually I stayed fairly near home, not going much farther than Greenham Park, or the canal. But one afternoon I became a little more ambitious and decided to walk to Enborne. We had often walked there for picnics so it was not beyond the energy of a nine-year-old. It was a pleasant afternoon, and in the bright sunshine the distance did not seem as great as I had thought it might. As I approached the narrow bridge a man came from the opposite direction leading a cart-horse, obviously a young farm labourer. We met.

"Do you want a banana?" he said.

I could see he had none so I took no notice, continuing my walk.

"Do you wanna ride on my horse?"

"No thank you." I called without looking back.

The trouble was that I was just here due to turn round and go home. The road ahead was unfamiliar but I had to keep going, as he had turned the horse and was now following me. There was no other soul in sight. By the time I was on the bridge, which is narrow, and walled on both sides, he had caught me up. He took me by the arm and turned me to face him. Escape was impossible. My right arm was rubbing the wall, and on the other side of me was more horse that I had ever been close to before, while facing me was the man. He then proceeded to expose himself, and invited my co-operation. Sheer disgust and panic gave me courage. I ducked under the great horse and out on to the road, and then I just ran for home. He could not give chase because he dared not leave his master's horse, so I was truly grateful to the huge, alarming animal. The two miles back were covered at a rapid scout's pace, and I tumbled indoors breathless, hot and half crying. Bit by bit I told the tale, with difficulty, having no language for the purpose, and was surprised to see my mother crying. She gave me lemonade and a rest on the sofa.

"I should forget all about it now, and don't tell your friends."

I did not want to.

That evening Daddy came into our bedroom to say goodnight.

"You won't go for any more walks on your own, will you Jane? It's a shame, but you mustn't. Promise?"

I promised, and obeyed.

I was in my second year when the High School, properly called the County Girls' Grammar School, (but also designated N.G.S. for Newbury Girls' School), had its twenty-fifth birthday celebrations. For this event I needed my mandatory tricoline dress.

I had heard from Laura and others about these 'best' school dresses, only worn on very special occasions. We had had a diagram included in our uniform list, but my mother wisely preferred to wait until it was called for before making one, in case I had outgrown it before it had ever been used. Now we were to have, amongst other things, a Parents' evening to celebrate our quarter century, with music and choral-speaking by the girls.

'Tricoline' was the brand name of a silky, firm, rustly material, somewhat like a mild taffeta. Our dresses were of white tricoline, not the modern, toned-down, off-white colour, but pure, dazzling snow-white, with black stockings. This produced a strange effect as we waited in semi-darkness for our turn to mount the stage en masse. The brilliant white was evident everywhere, but our black stockings merged into the darkness, and it seemed to me that our school was inhabited by a race of legless maidens. The effect of this solid phalanx of virgin purity must have been very satisfying to Governors, Staff and parents, but we all felt a bit silly in our 'trics'.

It was a boring concert for the small girls. We sang in unison, 'The Cock is Crowing', and 'Jerusalem', and that was our excitement over for the evening. My parents were not there. Mamma was ill, and Daddy never felt at home with what he called the 'gentry'. Neither of my parents ever set foot inside my school.

The outings and concerts I really enjoyed were those organised by our Sunday School, which was a large and flourishing one when we attended it. At the High School I was a very unimportant, very small person of doubtful origin. At Sunday School I was in the running for star parts and limelight. In my eight years at the High School I never took part in a single school play. I was nine when the Sunday School did 'Babes in the Wood', and I was the girl babe. This was a straight play, not a pantomime. It was most moving, especially when the two babes had to lie down and die of starvation and exposure, and three fat little birds in black plimsolls hopped in, chirping their best, and strewed us with dead leaves. Being strewn was a novel sensation for us as it was unrehearsed. No use making a mess for nothing! The birds failed in their first real attempt to cover us up, as the teachers pointed out.

"Well," protested the robin, hampered in speech by his cardboard beak, "all the leaves kept slipping off their bottoms."

The footlights were a row of acetylene lamps. I recollect that they had to be filled with a gritty, grey powder, lit with a match and turned up just before the performance. The result was a battery of such brilliance that the audience must have had a clearer view of our feet and ankles than of anything else on stage. The sweet, nauseating smell of acetylene worried me throughout the whole play, and remains a vivid memory within the senses to this day.

Our next play was the 'Sleeping Beauty', and this was memorable for its successful casting of characters. We seemed to have just the ideal child for each part, or so it seemed to me. The witch had dark, almond-shaped eyes and a beguiling smile. The Prince was tall and good-looking, and the three elves, who were mischievous schoolboys of my own age, were perfect in size and face. I was the good fairy, whose job it was to commute the death sentence into one of a century of sleep. But the Princess! When she had unplaited her long dark tresses and let them fall rippling to her waist, and when she then stepped into her long, white satin gown and put on her scintillating diamond crown, I simply could not believe that this was good old Elsie, who always chose gob-stoppers.

Our last play in my time was the best of all. It was a musical version of 'Aladdin' in four-beat rhymed couplets. We grew to like the songs from this play very much; they were simple, suitable, varied and tuneful, and I can still remember them. The show was spectacular for its costumes too. There were flower-fairies, tea-shop girls, (a simple version of geishas), an Emperor, (last year's Prince), a wonderful Dame Wishy-Washy and a fully turned out genie. Norma and Doreen were chrysanthemum fairies, and looked lovely. These splendid costumes were not hired, but were either made or lent by the Sunday School teachers, and by a few mothers.

The good singing in this play had been noted by the Choirmaster and the choir committee. They invited half a dozen boys and girls, all between ten and twelve years old to become choir members, and most of them accepted. So it was that I joined the Northbrook Street Church choir just before my eleventh birthday, and have been a member ever since. Our organist was a young man of twenty-five, energetic, enthusiastic, and possessing a charismatic personality. He fulfilled the exacting duties of playing the organ, not only on Sundays, but at weddings, funerals and at extra services during the week, and of training the choir, maintaining this unremitting service for a full fifty years, until his death. I little thought, as I sat nervously in the vestry that first day in my best clothes, what an important step in my life I had just taken.

Mamma, who spent most of her time in bed now, gave me a little talk on what was expected of a choir member. She and her sisters had sung in the choir there.

"It's going to make you a little tired on Friday mornings," (choir practice used to be on Thursdays then), "so you must get up cheerfully for school. No grumbling!"

"No, I shan't mind."

"You will have to be regular of course. They must know how many to expect each Sunday. And I think you ought to have a hat. All ladies wear hats in church."

They did at that time, but we, as children, did not.

The Methodist Church covered with Virginia Creeper

JOSEPH HOPSON & SONS. Furnishers, House Agents, Plumbers, Decorators, &c., Northbrook Street, Newbury.

Shops at the corner of West Street

Northbrook Street, Newbury

"Miss Laycock can take you down to Dexter Robinson's on Saturday, and you can choose one in the price range."

We set off on Saturday accordingly. I had never had a new hat as far as I could remember, except of course my uniform school hat the previous autumn. It did not take me long to choose. The size and the price cut down the choice to one or two, and from these I found one I liked very much. It was a smooth, thin straw, creamy coloured with a brim which faded away to nothing at the back. Regrettably I was too old for a circlet of little buttercups and forget-me-nots, but there was ribbon round it which ended in a neat bow. Mamma approved our choice.

This was my choir hat, and I was very proud of it. The ladies of the choir admired it and wished they had one like it. It seemed to add something to my stature. Each Sunday, after the evening service I brushed it round with the clothes brush and wrapped it in the tissue-paper in which I had carried it home. It stayed uncrushed all the week.

It was through becoming a choir member that I first learned the truth of the adage,

'Oh, what a tangled web we weave,
When first we practice to deceive.'

Brenda, who was also a choir 'nipper', had asked me to go to tea with her at her little cousin's house. The baby's mother was going out, and had asked Brenda and a friend to baby-sit.

I set out, wearing my choir hat, met Brenda and went with her to her Aunt's house. There we played with the baby very happily until her mother returned and gave us tea. Then we played again, and the time flew.

"It's six o'clock, Brenda. What about chapel?"

"I'm not going. Mamma said I needn't if I didn't want to."

I had not been told this, but I did not want to leave Brenda and her dear little cousin.

"Why don't you stay? They won't mind for once."

"Mamma doesn't know I'm not going. She'll think I'm there."

"Well, you can tell her after. She won't mind."

I was not sure about that. It seemed worse to disobey her because she was ill in bed. If I could have asked her first it would not have mattered, but I could not, and it was very tempting to skip chapel for once and stay and play with the baby. I stayed.

When I got home Mamma asked,

"Was it a good service?"

"Yes, thanks."

"Did Brenda go?"

"Well, she had to look after the baby, so we took her to chapel with us."

"Good heavens! Whatever did you do with a baby in the choir?"

"Well, we sat her in between us. She was ever so good, and didn't make a sound. No-one really knew she was there."

Oh dear!

"You should never have done that. Didn't anyone tell you off?"

"No." I could see no way of extricating myself now, and was bitterly regretting my first lie.

"Well, I think I must write them a note, through the Choir Secretary, to

89

to apologise for you both, and let them know that you will not do such a thing again."

I put away my choir hat with less than the usual pleasure, and passed the next few days in a cloud of dread. Had Mamma written the letter by now, and would all be revealed? I could not even gain comfort from confiding in Brenda. She had neither disobeyed nor told lies. I was the sinner.

The week-end came and went, and there was no evidence of a damning revelation. I was not expelled from the choir. There were neither hints nor recriminations. Mamma said no more about it, and I thankfully concluded she had taken no action in the matter. The whole incident was a moral lesson which I shall never forget.

CHAPTER TWENTY-TWO

I was out in the school field 'practising' for nothing, tossing the ball forward with the lacrosse stick and scooping it up, cradling it and tossing again, all for the benefit of the sharp-eyed games mistress, until at last I reached the shelter of the bushes in the open-air theatre. Then I gave up all pretence of practising.

To my surprise and delight Laura was there, with a lacrosse stick in her hands and a ball at her feet.

"Aren't you playing today?"

"Nope. She told me to go and practise for my second grade. I passed the first ages ago, and haven't bothered since."

These 'grades' were tests of skill for lacrosse players, and we were all, theoretically, supposed to be driving ourselves hard to pass the next one. This proved discouraging to most average players, because the sporty types who could do everything physical went through all the grades like a spoon through porridge. I had not even passed Grade One. Why bother?

We pushed the ball around a bit, to send our obliging consciences to sleep, and then fell to talking and laughing, in the midst of which we heard a screech of brakes just outside the main school gate.

"Whoops," said Laura, "bang-bang!"

We could not go over to have a look, right past the dedicated lacrosse-players and the games mistress, but we could see heads over the hedge, and a little crowd collecting. A moment later an ambulance arrived from the hospital just down the road.

"Looks as if someone's injured," Laura said. "Hope there's still some blood about when we go home."

The whistle blew. We wandered in, put away our lacrosse sticks and changed our shoes for prep. When we went home there was nothing at all to see.

Next morning at school we were met by the news that one of our girls had been killed. Cycling home with a friend she had turned to adjust her case on the back carrier and had run into a lorry. Prayers that morning were for some reason held in the gymnasium, and Miss Luker officially announced the tragedy from the platform. In future, she said, girls riding to school on bicycles were to ride singly, and never two abreast, as this had been the reason for the accident. A deep gloom pervaded the school for some days. The victim had been a cheerful, pretty girl, much liked by everyone.

Several months later Laura and I broke a school rule by buying sweets on our way to school, and what was worse, eating them. Worse still, they were licquorice bats, which were hard and chewy and long-lasting. But worst of all, as we approached the school gate a red car passed us, Miss Luker's car, with her driving and the deputy head sitting in the front with her. We shoved our licquorice bats into our top blazer pockets, cleaned ourselves with handkerchiefs and hoped for the best.

In vain! No sooner had the bell gone than we were sent for by the deputy head. We stood before her, feigning innocence.

"Come on," she said. "Where is it?"

Laura said, "What, Miss C?" and I, simultaneously, produced mine from my pocket. We had no concerted plan of action.

"That's right. You know what I'm after. Where's yours?"

Defeated, Laura produced hers.

"Revolting!" The deputy head made a moue of disgust. "Not only do you break school rules, but you do it in the worst possible way. Follow me."

We did, and found ourselves at the back of the kitchen where school meals were prepared. Lifting the lid of a dustbin she ordered,

"In there."

We dropped them in.

"No. Push them right down under the garbage."

We pushed them right down under the garbage.

"Do you realise that as well as breaking rules and giving our school a bad name you were behaving dangerously?"

This was news to us.

"There you were, crossing the road, chewing away, and not noticing the traffic. Have you so soon forgotten the little girl killed on this very road?"

My eyes filled with tears.

"No, I see you have not. Well, that's something in your favour. Wash your hands and get back to your class."

This we did, more than thankful to escape, but what a waste of a penny each!

Mamma was by now scarcely ever out of bed, and her activities were limited to doing the mending. She darned my black woollen stockings so neatly over the knees that they attracted the attention of my form-mistress. I did not notice any change in her condition. She seemed as cheerful and as conversational as ever.

One afternoon when I got in from school she was not there. She had gone for a little holiday in Reading with Auntie Rose and Uncle Tom. I missed her presence very much, and started again on a long wait for her return.

The days passed. Daddy cycled to Reading on Sundays to visit her. Just occasionally he went on the bus, but he did not take any of us with him. Mamma always sent her love.

Miss Laycock carried on housekeeping. Several times a week she gave us stew for dinner, which contained lots of haricot beans and carrots, but very little meat. We liked it well enough, but grew very tired of it. Another food we wearied of was scones. Miss Laycock never cooked cakes, but produced scones by the stone. It was certainly not her fault that money was scarce, but she had no imagination and no initiative, and our meals were very dull and of poor nutritional content.

One of the worst quarrels I ever had with her was at the table. She had just told us that one of her aunts used to make her children have pudding first and meat after.

"Why?" I naturally wanted to know.

"Because they wasn't wantin' so much meat after." She laughed at the devilish cleverness of this ruse.

"Well, why didn't she just give them their share of meat first, and then give them their pudding?"

"Don't you be cheeky. My auntie knowed what she was doing. Don't you start on about her, little Miss Clever!"

"I'm not. But it just seems the sensible thing to do."

"That's enough of it! My auntie had more sense in her head than you'll ever have, with all your highty-tighty schooling!"

I stood my ground verbally until she stood up to put me down, and then we had a pitched battle. She won, just, but I was growing fast and it was clear that she would not have the physical advantage for much longer.

It would never have occurred to her to apologise. For one thing, in her book an adult did not apologise to a child, and in any case, she thought that she was in the right. But I could not live for long in a fog of disapproval. Following the exhilaration of battle came the depression of guilt, and a restless desire to put things right.

"I'm sorry, Miss Laycock."

Her brown, bony arms grabbed me to her in a hard clutch, pressing my face against her nigger-brown, crepe-de-chine dress which smelt of sweat. I struggled to free myself, further disturbed by this alarming glimpse of the ferocity of possessive love.

I could not appeal to Daddy for support. He was absorbed in worry, and in any case he would not have known what to do. Someone had to be in charge of us all. He had no wish to weaken her authority, and risk her leaving us. So Miss Laycock and I quarrelled, and made it up, and things muddled on.

By the end of that September there was a tension in the house. I was scared of Daddy. He was so distant and withdrawn, and hardly ever spoke to us. The smaller children did not seem to notice it, and Lucy, being away at school, did not know.

On Saturday morning he came into our bedroom before we were up, and just stood there, rubbing the knob of the bed-post and saying nothing, yet he did not go. He needed help.

"How's Mamma, Daddy?"

There was a pause.

"I'm afraid you haven't got a Mamma any more." He just turned and went out.

I shed a few tears, for decency's sake, and Norma and Doreen cried with me, but I was not really ready for crying. I was angry, angry with fate.

It had happened, as I had long known it must. Our mother had died, leaving Lucy, fourteen, me, twelve, Norma, eight, Doreen, six, and Patrick, barely three years old.

It was October again.

Quite soon after my mother's death another plot was hatched to get me into hospital for the tonsils operations, and this time there was no escape.

During the Easter holiday Lucy received a letter from Auntie Edith, back now as a theatre sister in the South London Hospital for women. She asked her to find a mauve dressing-gown which she had left in a cupboard and to cut it down to fit me. Also to check that my nighties and under-clothes were in order. I thought how kind of her it was to give me her dressing-gown! I had never had one before.

Lucy then surprised me again by her boldness. She got out Mamma's sewing-machine, threaded it up and proceeded to stitch.

"Are you allowed?" I asked, biting a finger nail.

"If I'm old enough to do grown-up jobs for people I'm old enough to use the machine. There's no-one else to use it, is there?"

Her logic, as usual, was perfect. She made a good job of the dressing-gown.

Daddy told me the next day that I was going to spend a few days in London with Auntie Edith. I instantly thought of the zoo, and Buckingham Palace.

"Don't get too excited." Lucy warned.

By the time of departure some inkling of the truth was trickling through. I did not want to go.

"Why do I have to go?" I wailed. "I'll miss all my Easter holiday with Lucy."

"Don't worry. There will be plenty more holidays to come." Daddy told me.

I was put on the Paddington train, alone, and told to wait on the platform upon arrival.

"The train doesn't go any farther," Daddy said, "so you can't possibly go past." This was my great worry. In spite of assurances I felt very anxious as the end of the journey drew near. Whatever would I do if no-one was there to meet me?

Auntie Edith was there on the platform and found me without difficulty. We went off the station and had a meal in a Lyon's cafe, and I felt we were living it up.

After that we went to an outfitter's and she bought me a navy-blue beret to match the navy school coat I was wearing, as the spring wind was blowing cold.

"I'm taking you now to the hospital where I work, and to see a specialist about your tonsils. You won't mind, will you, because I'm coming with you."

So we saw the specialist, a woman, and Auntie explained that this lady had kindly found a bed for me in her hospital. We went into the ward.

"If one of the nurses offers you a bath, Jane, just accept it, won't you? Don't say, "I had mine yesterday", because some people have a bath every day you see."

I had heard of such people, and I like to think that I did not need the tactful warning. But I promised to do as she asked.

The ward in which I found myself was unusual. It consisted of a long corridor on either side of which were small separate bedrooms, with a curtain over the entrance instead of a door. There were no crevices in these rooms. Wall met floor and ceiling on a curve, and there were no corners or joins where dust could accumulate. My bed-side locker was already friendly-looking with a story book, a vase of daffodils and a box of chocolate neapolitans.

I could not sleep that night. The ward was light, and noisy compared with home, and I was nervous. Towards dawn I dozed off, and then was awakened very early with a bowl of water to wash in. During the morning a doctor arrived and carried out the routine pre-operative tests, after which I was allowed to go into the day-room. This was a very small and rather dark room with a sofa and two arm-chairs, and a very small coal fire. I sat on the sofa in my mauve dressing-gown between two ladies who talked all the time about their operations. There was nothing to do, so I went back to my bed and my book.

The next morning the nurse brought me a very weak cup of tea with no sugar.

"No breakfast for you this morning, because of your operation."

I did hope it would be soon, as I was very hungry.

Before long the same nurse came and dressed me in some most peculiar clothes and a funny cotton hat, and I lay and waited for the next thing to happen. Auntie Edith came in to see me.

"They'll be fetching you soon to take you down to the operating theatre. You needn't be frightened because I'll be there to hold your hand."

There was a rumbling sound along the corridor, like a tumbril, and the stretcher arrived. Two men in white jackets lifted me from the bed.

"Can't I walk there?" I begged. "I'd much rather walk."

"Sorry, my dear, not allowed." said one of the men. "This is the way it has to be."

So off we trundled, the tiny, solid wheels moving in close contact with the unyielding concrete floor sending a sizzle of minute tremors through my whole body. The operating theatre really was a frightening place. There were no pre-operative injections to induce drowsiness at that time. One was plunged wide-eyed into the very scene of the deed. I saw Auntie Edith, but she was wearing a mask and gown, so if she smiled at me I did not see it. True to her word she held my hand whilst the dreadful mask came down over my face, suffocating and evil-smelling. I struggled to free myself for breath, but my hands were now pinioned tightly against my sides.

"Traitor!" I thought. "You traitor!"

My panic grew to an acute, intolerable pitch. There was a buzzing in my ears, and a bright star appeared in the distance from out of an unbelievable darkness and stench. It came nearer, and grew bigger, alarmingly bright, until the great darkness engulfed me.

I have had two experiences of a general anaesthetic since that first time, but now that the face mask is not used it is no longer so terrifying. What has not changed, for me, is the return to consciousness.

I was aware, out of the total blackness and annihilation, of a sudden surge of sound, and before I was able to account for it I was unconscious again. This happened several times, without my having any idea of the amount of time which had elapsed between the surges. Then came the realisation that the sounds were those of the hospital ward; I knew where I was, and had a sudden distinct awareness that there was a 'me' somewhere in the midst of it all. Light began to assail my eyes, and by opening them I could see people and things, but the room, although familiar, seemed different.

Auntie Edith was there when I came round, in her uniform but without the mask. After a few minutes she said,

"I must go now. I'm supposed to be on duty."

A bad day followed, and a bad night. I had a very high temperature, raging headache, and was parched with thirst but unable to swallow anything. The nurse, before going off duty for the night, had brought in a glass, and a jug of lemondade. Merely to look at it was torture, as I could not drink any, although I was constantly urged to try.

Recovery was slow, but normal. On the third day, when I really was feeling a bit better the nurse said,

"I'm sending a little girl in to see you. She's the same age as you and she's just had her tonsils out too."

This was Pat, a doctor's daughter from Hounslow, who padded into my room in her blue dressing-gown and pretty slippers. We got on very well, and her visit passed the time happily. She came to see me twice a day. I was surprised that she was walking about and eating everything, whilst I was kept in bed and having such difficulty in swallowing.

Pat went home after five days, and I missed her very much. I hoped my discharge would be soon. Auntie Edith came in to see me whenever she went off duty. She had been 'carpeted' by Matron for being at my bed-side when I had come back from the operation, when she should have been on duty in the theatre.

I left the hospital after eight days, and we went by train to Reading, where another taxi took us to Auntie Rosie's house. Here I was to stay for a few days' convalescence, as there was no-one at home to look after me properly.

Auntie Rosie had a bed ready for me, with a hot water bottle, and I was glad to creep in and rest. I had strange thoughts about this bed, the only spare one in the house. Later on Auntie brought up a tray with high tea, grapefruit, boiled egg and bread and butter, chocolate cake and a cup of tea, all of which I ate with enjoyment. There was a parcel for me from my Sunday School teacher, a book about King Arthur's Knights, and a letter. I began to fear I would be spoiled.

When she came in to collect the tray Auntie Rosie said,

"Edith has gone on to Newbury to see Grandma, and she's going to take Lucy out for the day before she goes back to school. She hasn't had much fun this holiday without you."

After a few days I went back to Newbury, and was glad to be home. Lucy was still there, I was pleased to find.

"Aren't you thin?" were her first words.

"Am I?" I had not noticed. "That's because I couldn't eat anything for ages."

Lucy told me all about her day at the zoo, and I told her of my adventures. There were not many days left of the holiday.

Sunday came round, and I got ready for Church as usual. It was a warm May day, so I thought I would wear my lovely choir hat. I removed the tissue paper with care and anticipation. Then I received a shock. The crown was soft and squashy, the brim as wavy as a range of hills, the ribbon spotted and patchy.

"Look what's happened to my best hat in the winter." I called to Lucy, who had been watching from a distance, twisting her hair.

She laughed, nervously, not cruelly.

"The rain did that," she said. "I wore it to the zoo. Auntie told me to."

"You shouldn't have done that, you had no right to wear my things. I don't wear yours!"

"I'm sorry. Auntie thought I looked nice in it. She was very sorry too. I pressed the brim with a warm iron, but it wouldn't go straight."

"Well, I'm not wearing that! I'll have to wear my school hat, that's all, and no-one else wears their school hat to church."

"Why don't you go without one? Some ladies do, and lots of girls."

I thought about it. Then I remembered Mamma saying, 'All ladies wear hats in church'.

"I'll wear my school one."

"What about your new beret? That looks nice."

I had forgotten the beret, and it solved the problem. Our generation, as it grew up, gradually rejected the church hat for ladies, so that those who still do wear one do it from personal preference.

CHAPTER TWENTY-THREE

There was a dullness about my life since our mother had died, due to the final removal of hope. The future seemed an endless perspective of grey days, with home dominated by Miss Laycock, and school standards leaving me lagging behind. From the point of view of the staff I was in every respect unsatisfactory, untidy in my uniform, unruly in class, and unconscientious in my work. And yet I loved to learn. I was avidly reading all of Dickens's works, some of George Eliot's, the novels of Harrison Ainsworth, anything available.

I was writing poetry at this time, mostly at home, but occasionally by order from school. I wrote a novel called 'The Rough Diamond', about a girl whom nobody liked, and no-one believed in, who nevertheless turned out well. It was bound in leather, by me. At the same time I made a small leather-covered note-book, (obviously someone had given me some odd bits of leather), and in this I secretly kept little scraps of poems and novels which I especially liked. There were some of the more mordant passages from 'Oliver Twist', selections from 'Romola', and a long excerpt from Andrew Marvell's 'Thoughts in a Garden' . . .

'What wondrous life is this I lead, . . .'

Lucy still often acted as my educational mentor. She used to recommend books for me to read.

"Have you read 'Hard Times'?"

"No."

"You should. It's a very good book."

"Have you read it?"

"No, but it's a book you ought to read. Our English mistress said so."

Another was 'Mark Twain'. Lucy had not read it, but was emphatic that, to be properly educated, one should. I was willing to read anything available, so vicariously, the Christ's Hospital English teacher was educating an unknown pupil.

During this grey period my great standby was Guiding, and the friendship with Meg which had deepened through our mutual enthusiasm for everything appertaining to Guides. It was a beneficial interest, which took us out and about, and developed our abilities. At school I was till 'persona non grata'; at Guides very much the opposite.

With the return of spring and better weather out came our pair of stilts, and with it the recollection of the I. C. Of course Meg now wanted to join.

"It's a pity we haven't got a headquarters," I said to her, "so we could meet when it rains." I thought wistfully of the vast area of the drill hall, where we held our Guide meetings.

Meg and I were in our garden, it was the Easter holiday.

"Let's look in our shed," I said, "It might do."

We looked inside. It was a good shed, but one corner was given over to lengths of wood stood against the wall. Another corner contained a heap of sawdust and wood shavings. Tools for carpentry and for gardening occupied nearly all the walls. Daddy's work-bench and vice ran the whole length of one side. The only blank space was the space for his bike to lean when he was home from work, as he always would be in the evenings when we held our meetings. It was undeniably a little cramped for a go-ahead Ideas Club.

"We could have it in our shed," Meg announced. "I'll ask Daddy. I'm sure he'll let us."

So our club moved to new premises. Meg's shed was no bigger, but it was a better shape, and much emptier. This move, and the fact that we were all a year older slightly changed the character of the club. It became more heavily organised, and underwent a turnover of membership. The old faithfuls were still there, Lucy and I, Laura and Jeanie, and now Meg, but we lost some of the others and gained new ones.

We thought we might have a token uniform. I suggested we could make hats like our camp hats, with a badge, but this proved too difficult for us. We did weave badges, with wool over card, embroidered I. C. on the front and affixed a safety pin at the back.

Our best idea, which was to have a sleeve, originated in the Guide uniform. The Guide proficiency badges had to be stitched to the right sleeve, starting from the cuff. If we each make a sleeve to wear, club members could also take tests and win badges.

It took us most of the summer to organise this, meeting weekly in Meg's shed. By the time we had decided upon the type of test and made the badges to award the summer was well advanced. We did have time to run a knitting test, which everyone passed, and a singing test, which opened up a problem, since the judges were also competitors.

Most of us had clear, tuneful voices, and were judged to have passed. When Jeanie's turn came she could only produce a hoarse, throaty performance.

"Jeanie hasn't passed." I announced. "Her voice is not good enough."

"That's not fair," she protested. "You know I've got asthma. It's not my fault."

"No, I know it's not, but we've got to judge properly."

"My teacher said I would be a good singer if I didn't get asthma. I would be just as good as you lot. It's not fair."

"We're not saying it is fair, Jeanie, but if everyone passes everthing even when they can't do it it's a waste of time having tests at all."

"If I don't pass I shall leave the club, and so will Laura, won't you Laura?"

Poor Laura was in a dilemma. She could see the justice of her sister's claim, but did not want to lose face with the club, even less to leave it.

"I should let her pass, and just put 'A' for asthma by her name in the book, else Mum will think we're picking on her."

And so the problem was solved, although I still felt we had opened the door to a lowering of standards.

Although I enjoyed singing so much myself it was during the class music lessons that I was at my most disruptive. These lessons were unadventurous and dull. We did no part-singing at all, and the class produced only a faint and feeble unison. But I was only a nuisance to the teachers, no more. The school went on in its orderly way despite my peccadilloes.

But I was not impervious to the school's influences. Miss Luker, along with others of her staff selected some very inspiring hymns for the school assembly. I found myself responding with a lift of spirit to Johnson's

'Life of ages, richly poured, love of God unspent and free,
Flowing in the prophet's word, and the people's liberty.'

As practical evidence of idealism the school became, in 1930, a corporate member of the League of Nations, and we read the handbook in class as a study in world affairs. It seemed to us that we had here the answer, and I gave my ready support to League of Nations activities. The collapse of the League, in 1939, was my first taste of real international disillusion.

The school took a serious interest in philanthropic work. We supported a London mission at Camberwell, and in a big way. Each form had to elect a mission monitress, whose task it was to collect from each girl a minimum 'gift' of twopence a term. More of course was hoped for. This produced a useful cheque to be sent to the Canon at the end of each year. An annual Mission Day was held, usually on a Friday in November, when gifts of every kind were brought to school and displayed on lockers and tables. These might be good quality used clothing, new garments, cakes, vegetables, a motley selection. The girls were allowed to file past to look at the gifts, form by form.

The next day being Saturday, some of the older girls went to school to sort and pack the things, which had to be arranged in layers in sacks, which were then stitched with string and a sacking needle, and clearly labelled, then dispatched to Camberwell. The cost of transport was slight considering the amount sent, making the effort economically worth while.

In 1930 came the terrible economic depression which cast its shadow over much of that decade. We were fairly fortunate. My father was a good workman, and since he had five children he was only once out of work, and not for long.

Many Newbury people were out of work, and the 'dole' was not enough to give a satisfactory standard of living. The office was in West Mills, just behind the Parish Church, and I can remember walking along Bartholomew Street and passing a long, long queue of men waiting on the pavement with hands in their empty pockets. My father took a photograph of it, an ironic picture with the lovely church as its background. He little thought that one day he would be a part of that queue, instead of an observer.

But it happened. He was unemployed for about six weeks during the depression's trough. He did some gardening, some carpentry, some violin playing, some reading.

We really did feel the pinch then, and it seemed to me that we never quite caught up again.

As Christmas came around that year the Round Table organised a party in the Corn Exchange for children of the unemployed. We had tickets for it but Daddy was not keen for us to go.

"Do let me, Daddy. Look, it says, 'Presents for all'."

So I went. There was a good tea, and an entertainment, followed by games, but there was something odd about this party. It was not a friend's party, or a choir party, or a Sunday School party. Amongst the hundreds of children present there was no common cause. They were all just children whose fathers were out of work. I only recognised a face here and there. It was not the sort of party I was used to.

But the parcels were huge! They were not personally labelled, of course, but were divided into four piles. Then the children were sorted into four files, boys under seven, boys over seven, and girls likewise, so we each received the right type of parcel. It was a wonderful feat of generosity and organisation. I clutched my enormous string-tied parcel and ran home to see what was inside.

I had a momentary pang as the contents were revealed. They were not new. They had been collected by the Round Tablers to help children who 'would not get much for Christmas this year'. Nevertheless they were unbroken, acceptable toys. There was a doll, several story books, a jig-saw puzzle and some beads for threading, and I was delighted.

"Look, Daddy. Look at all these presents!"

"Well done, my dear," was all he had to say. He had been a widower scarcely two months, and was not talkative. I also detected another overtone, pride.

We children made our own happiness that Christmas, but it was a shadowed happiness. It might have been very bleak indeed, but for the unfailing kindness of friends.

When the spring came Daddy got a job at Tring, Herts. This meant that he had to find lodgings there, and was only home at weekends. His only means of transport was the bicycle. It did not seem very long, however, before he was again able to get work in Newbury, and things became once more as normal as they were ever likely to be.

We had several times asked Daddy when Patrick was going to start school as he was now five, and he replied that there was plenty of time. By the time Easter had come we had persuaded him that Patrick really should go to school, and we ought to book him in. The nearest Infant school for Patrick was St. John's Church of England School in Newtown Road. The headmistress here had been one of our teachers in the Infant department of the Council School. It was agreed that Lucy and I should go and see her.

So, somewhat to her surprise, we turned up on her private doorstep one afternoon in the Easter holiday to ask her if Patrick could start in the summer term. She suggested that we should bring him along to school on the first day of term.

It was a strange direction for us to take, starting as we had always done by going over the Rockingham Road railway bridge and along Pound Street, where they were already pulling down the old Rectory, but turning right at the umbrella shop, which is now a private house. Lucy and I were always intrigued by this dark little shop with its bow windows and total lack of customers. We walked past the 'Litten', which during my lifetime has been used as offices, and before that as a typewriting school, and earlier still as a private school for young children. It is now carefully restored for use as offices again.

The 'Litten' was founded as a hospital in about 1200, one of King John's few good deeds, and together with the ancient and well-maintained almshouses behind it, has served the community as a charity until quite recently. Across the street from the 'Litten' we passed the black iron railings of the 'meadow', where St. Bartholomew's Fair was held annually when I was small. We always considered that this was a second, and less important fair, and never went to it. The really good fair was the Michaelmas Fair, in November, originally held in the Market Place until it grew and overflowed into the Wharf, and all along Cheap Street as far as the junction with Market Street. Having reached this dimension and bursting bonds in all directions a new venue was found for it, on Northcroft Field.

But we were taking Patrick to school. We reached the cross-road which is now a roundabout, and on the other side was the modest, grey stone building of St. John's Church, where now the modern brick church makes an imposing landmark. Opposite to it stood a neat row of small almshouses with little front gardens. Both church and almshouses were destroyed in a daylight air-raid in February 1943. With Lucy and me carefully holding Patrick's hands we crossed the busy Andover Road by the hospital and arrived at the already old school of St. John, originally a Sunday school, and which, with the exception of St. Nicholas' School, is the oldest in Newbury. This is where Patrick started school, and was happy, and made rapid progress.

CHAPTER TWENTY-FOUR

Summer came round again, and this was to be the summer of the high jump. Not very high jumps, but better than we had so far been able to do.

Lucy and I played at jumping for several days, hoping to improve our peformance. We followed the standard procedure of tying the end of our rope to the fence, and holding the other end in the hand, thus taking turns to do the jumping. We tried to measure how high we cleared it, and squabbled because it dipped in the middle, which meant that Lucy, who jumped sideways, claimed to be jumping over the higher stretch, whilst I, a forward jumper, went straight through the 'dip'.

"If we had jumping stands like the school ones we would really know how high we're getting."

Simultaneously, it seemed, there wafted into our heads an image of all those straight pieces of timber resting against the wall in the corner of the shed. Without a word we dived in.

We soon had a pair of stands on fairly effective bases. Then came the tricky business of calibration, allowing an inch for the thickness of the base. Having marked off the inches with a pencil, we looked around and found the brace and bit to make the holes. Botheration and drat! The stands would not lie on the bench because of the wooden base. Even by putting the base off the edge of the bench we could not manage, because it was not then possible to move the wooden bar up and down the bench where we could work on it. Nothing for it but to take off the base, and put it on again when we had finished.

All this took more time than we had anticipated. We were longing to get jumping, but there were still the numbers to be written, and some pegs to make which would fit the holes. We found that twigs would do for these.

At last we were ready, and we set them up in the garden. The rope sagged between the stands as badly as ever.

"Well, of course it does," Lucy pointed out. "The school rope has a weight on each end."

We found two big stones, put them into squares of material and tied them tightly to the ends of our rope. Success at last! The day was over, but there was tomorrow, and tomorrow and tomorrow.

For the rest of the holiday we practised daily, and improved a little. Norma and Doreen and Patrick wanted to jump as well. The two younger girls made fast progress, and were threatening to catch us up. None of us was Olympics material, but we did learn a lot about the various methods of jumping, and about how and how not to land, and we had a wonderful few weeks of fun and competitive exercise.

Daddy eventually made us a bar, to be used instead of a rope, and some more efficient pegs. This gave us far more accurate records, and we were a little unchoughed to find that our real achievements were lower than we had thought, but it was the same for all of us, and we had to accept it.

The holiday came to an end; Lucy went tearfully back to school, and the autumn term shook itself into place with a clatter. I was fourteen, and was now in the lower fifth, which was definitely upper school. This was my school certificate year, so I determined to work hard, but my determination did not include any sacrifices. I was still an enthusiastic Guide, a choir member, a Guild member and a member of the Senior Sunday School.

Except for mathematics, which I found difficult, I enjoyed the school work.

Another fresh experience was in store, and one which proved to be a life-long fascination. We learned to use the microscopes.

They stood around the laboratory, and I had looked at them often, knowing what they were, and wondering how they worked. This year we were taught to use them. The science mistress demonstrated, and then got us all to look into it and to focus to our own sight. She showed us salt crystals, sugar crystals, a cut leaf section, a human hair.

"Now one of the most interesting things to observe through a microscope is pond water. I want you each to bring some next week in a jar."

"Shall we strain it?" someone asked.

"That would be a bit stupid, wouldn't it, if you're going to look for something? No, bring the smelly old stuff just as it is. A bit of mud from the bottom won't hurt."

"Where's the nearest pond?" I asked at home.

"There's Wash Common and the Marsh." Miss Laycock said.

"But the one in Enborne Road is the nearest." Norma said. "I'll come with you."

So the three of us went, Doreen, Norma and myself. It was only five minutes walk away.

"Mind you watch out. It's a hawful ol' pond."

Miss Laycock was right. It was an awful old pond. It lay in a hollow with sloping sides, and it was stagnant enough for any biologist. Tiny, round, green leaves lay undisturbed over its surface, except where the sheet was broken up by protruding petrol cans, motor tyres and old bikes.

"Ugh!" that was Doreen's reaction. "You can get some better water in the canal. Let's go."

Norma held her nose and said, "Pooh, what a pong!" and giggled. We all had to be careful not to slip down the scree and join the old bicycles. There was a broken, sad-looking willow tree growing close by, which had clearly been used as we now intended to use it.

"If you hold on to that branch, Norma, and hold my hand, I'll reach out and dip."

I collected a good jarful, and then we set off for home, not sorry to leave the smelly, depressing spot.

"Do you know," I told them, in an educating, big-sisterly sort of voice, "that three men were burnt there once?"

"What, in the water?" Doreen asked incredulously.

"No. There wasn't any water there then. It was a sandpit, and three men who would not give up their beliefs were tied to stakes and burnt."

"Cor! I bet that hurt!" Doreen and Norma were impressed.

"I wouldn't be as brave as that, would you?"

"I doubt it. Lots of people who saw them burn admired them, and thought their ideas must have been right after all."

"Who were they?"

"Julius Palmer, Thomas Askew and John Guin. There's a memorial to them in the prims' church, you know, opposite Inch's. I've seen it."

My pondwater was wonderfully rich in all the things the biology mistress had expected. We found paramoecium, amoeba, and my old friend of the swimming-pool, spirogyra. There were other fascinating things whose names I have forgotten. I could have looked into the microscope all day, but there was theory to be done, and notes to be made.

Since the day when my sisters and I collected the pondwater from the 'Martyrs' Sandpits' the site had become even more unrecognisable. The pond, and surrounding waste land were filled, and raised to a higher level by a hard core of prepared garbage. This went on for several unsightly years. The land was then left to consolidate, and eventually built over.

The Primitive Methodist Church has also disappeared. In 1933, when Methodist Union took place it had become Bartholomew Street Methodist Church, much loved and well-supported, with what had been excellent premises. Its frontage was enclosed by black iron railings marking the inside of the pavement, and just behind the railings was a board which displayed the frequently changed 'Wayside Pulpit'. These pithy sayings always appealed to me.

Opposite to this church was Inch's, the drapers, a family business which has meant a lot to Newbury for many years. It was sad to see it closed recently, and undergoing restoration for a different purpose. We girls used to gaze in stupefaction at the breadth of some of its outsize garments displayed in the window. One article was dubbed by us 'the biggest pair of knickers in the world'.

It was during the year 1933, when I was taking the Oxford School Certificate that the discovery was made that the Parish Church roof was in grave danger from death watch beetle. An appeal was made to the people of Newbury who responded magnificently. The town broke out in a rash of events to raise money. Dances were held, sports organised, fetes sprang up in the green fields all around our town, raffles and competitions of all kinds kept us agog with expectation.

The major event in which all the townsfolk were engaged in one gigantic production was the 'Olde Englishe Faire', held in the Market Place. The various stalls and side-shows were built as shops in a miniature old English small town, all grouped around the terra-cotta Queen Victoria and her terra-cotta lions. Trade was brisk as all the goods were home produced, fruit and vegetables, bread and confectionary, local needlework and knitting, carpentry and craft work of all kinds. There was ice-cream, of course, and balloons, and even one or two fairground attractions.

The whole town must have had an afternoon off work I think, juding by the size of the crowd, brightened by a goodly sprinkling of High School summer hats. This is worth mention since we were always strongly dissuaded from going to fairs, Woolworth's, and other such crowded places, especially in school uniform. But to this we were allowed, even urged, to go. I think that we too, must have had time off from school, because it was certainly an afternoon when I was there.

This delightful fair is always associated in my mind with a time of anxiety. Some little girls at school had been discovered passing round dirty drawings and notes, and the witch hunt was on. I was an innocent myself even at fourteen, and had little idea what form this pornography took, but it distressed me on two counts. Firstly, if a small child at our school could do such things, what must be the condition of the world at large? Secondly, there was a lot of chat about expulsion, and with past offences in mind, mightn't I be a candidate? Even though I was no longer a pest, my reputation remained. There was a general feeling of anxiety throughout the school.

Once the culprits had been found and reprimanded, and the edges of crime sealed up, the headmistress took a slightly self-conscious positive step to skew our minds in another direction. At precisely half past eleven on one particular morning every child in the school was given a slip of paper and was asked to write a list of the ten most beautiful things she could think of, no easy matter straight off the cuff! Going home a little later we discussed this strange task and compared our lists. One of my friends had included the new Parish Church roof, which I decided I really must go and see, so perhaps the 'purge' was not entirely wasted. But I was still left wondering what those drawings were about.

Laura had told me what she knew, which was not all, of the facts of life. Most children of my generation were left to find out about sex as best they could. I had no-one to teach me, as the following small incident shows.

Summer had brought its usual quota of white cabbage butterflies, darting from plant to plant dealing disaster. I was using a fishing net to collect a few specimens. Having made a capture I transferred it to the jar, and was amazed at what I saw.

"Miss Laycock! Miss Laycock!" I yelled, rushing indoors with my treasure. "Guess what I've caught. A double butterfly!"

Had my father been there he would have said,

"I don't think so, my dear. It's two single ones resting together."

and my mother would certainly have told me, at that age,

"It's a male and a female mating."

But Miss Laycock took one glance into the jar and went into peals of maniacal and knowing laughter. Stuffing her handkerchief into her mouth she ran into the other room, rubbing away her tears with the heels of her palms. For a moment I stood watching her, puzzled and irritated, then I took my double butterfly back out into the garden.

My fights with her continued, to the anxiety and admiration of the younger children, who admired my bravery, but I wondered how I dared. When I was about fourteen the fights became less frequent as we were more evenly matched, and battles of words took their places. Here I was at an obvious advantage, so she produced a verbal weapon which I could not counter.

It was a Saturday, and I was ready with my coat on to go and see Meg when Miss Laycock threw my black stockings over the table to me. I always darned my own stockings now.

"There you are. Get those done."

"Not now. I'll do them later."

"Now! You'll do them now."

"I can't. I'm going to Meg's. I can do them when I come in."

"Don't you defy me! I won't stand for it. You killed your mother. She died through you and your bad, wicked ways. It's you as killed her!"

I just left the house, deserting the field of battle. When she began in this vein in front of the other children I never stayed to hear her out. This was her biggest gun, and the one she always wheeled out when she found herself obviously losing the argument. That she knew it to be untrue was proved by the particular tenderness she showed me once her temper had cooled. She knew she had been cruel, and wanted to make amends, but I could not by then accept tenderness from her.

We had never been allowed to swear at home, in fact we knew very few swear words in those pre-television days. Therefore when under temporary stress and in need of a rich expletive I generally made one up. The word of the month happened to be 'blogger'.

I was on my way up the stairs where Miss Laycock was going round with a dust mop when I tripped and fell on my hands.

"Oh, blogger!"

"Don't you let me hear you saying them swear words in this house, Jane, or I'll tell your father."

"That's not swearing. I only said 'blogger'. I made it up."

"Yes it is swearing, and you knows it is. It's one of the most ungodliest words you can say. What would your mother have said?"

"She wouldn't have minded, because she would have known I'd made it up. You look in the dictionary. You won't find it, because I invented it."

"Oh, no you didn't! I heard you, you wicked, ungodly girl! It's no wonder she died, with you and your wickedness." etc. etc.

- But I did not stop to listen to any more.

CHAPTER TWENTY-FIVE

With the school certificate in sight we had, of course, more homework to do, and I was more inclined to take it seriously. But it was very difficult at home to settle down to work with the other three children there, all playing in the same room. Norma was now ten, Doreen eight and Patrick five. The girls were not in bed much before nine o'clock. Daddy was usually playing his violin in the sitting-room, and everything else went on in the living-room. Our bedroom had no table at which I could work, and in any case it was a shared room.

"Why don't you go to the Library Reading Room?" Daddy suggested.

"They've got lovely great tables to spread your books out, and it's quiet there."

It seemed a good idea, and I went there quite often. I already had tickets as a borrower, so my face was familiar to the Staff. I had read quite a number of novels from the shelves and enjoyed them, in spite of the dark and daunting bindings which made them all look alike. When handled separately these books were a pleasure, because they were heavily and handsomely bound, but their collective darkness further darkened a room which was by no means light to start with.

I found that the quietness, too, was a comparative, rather than a positive state in the reading room. A large notice over the entrance said 'Silence', and in deference to this no-one spoke. But the newspapers were all displayed on stands around the room, and were always well patronised, and the sound of a dozen people turning large papers over and over reached quite a high decibel count. There were also tramps who appreciated the quietness, the warmth, and the seats to sit on, and the highly polished tables whereon to lay their heads.

Flitting happily between the bookshelves was someone I knew, a young, golden-haired girl who had left school the previous year. Helen Purvis had been a keen and competent librarian at the High School, and was now starting upon her life's work among books.

The reading room was a great help to me. I felt sad when the Library was remodelled, and the original front door filled in. The result is a bigger and more easily run library, but I like to remember the old, dark, and slightly mysterious place it once was.

The examinations began early in July. On the day they started Miss Luker called me to her room after break. I attended in fear and trembling.

"I hope you have explained to your father, Jane, that you are only taking a sporting chance this year. You are very young to attempt the school certificate."

I said yes, I had told him. In reality I had never discussed it with him at all. That evening Daddy and I were having our supper together, bread and cheese and cocoa. This was normal; the children were all in bed, and we were alone. I was still revising history notes as I drank my cocoa.

"Put it away now, my dear. You've done enough for tonight."

I put the books away in my satchel.

"We start our exams tomorrow, Daddy."

"Well, good luck! Do your best."

He had no idea that this was a public examination, that all the other girls were in a ferment, and their parents too, getting them off to bed early, filling their fountain pens, sharpening their pencils, giving them last words of advice and snacks for between exams.

I sighed, and filled my own pen. Might as well go to bed now. I can't learn any more. Shan't pass anyway.

At a little before nine-thirty the next morning we were all standing in line outside the hall door, armed with a pen, pencil, rubber and ruler. The doors opened and we filed in, taking our places at the named desks, set well apart. Headings first, then the papers were laid before us, face downwards.

"Turn your papers over. You may begin."

And so it went on for a fortnight, with the concomitant shocks and despair, delight and depression so familiar to all schoolchildren. At last it was over and we left everything thankfully in the lap of the gods.

We had been told to look in the 'Times' or the 'Guardian' on September 1st. for results, as candidates were not individually notified then. My name was there. I had passed, but for more details we all had to wait until we were back at school and were sent for one by one to the headmistress's study. Being now a post-school certificate girl I was automatically in the Upper V, a very small form of about ten pupils. All the rest had left. I was now what I had once called a 'big bug', and most anxious to prove worthy.

Still with me in Upper V was Gina, the mousy girl who had started in the same form as me eight years ago. It was natural that we should now draw closer together, with such a build-up of shared experience. Gina was a girl with an attractive personality and a pleasant voice. She lived in a farm-house in a nearby village, and during this time we visited each other's houses a good deal. Gina was more mature than I was, and she already had a boy-friend.

"I saw him last night, Jane! All I saw was the back of him in the Market Place, but my knees went so weak I could hardly make it to the bus-stop."

She tried to explain to me what it was like to be in love.

"Haven't you ever been in love, Jane?" asked this pale seventeen-year-old who attracted the boys like flies to a honey pot.

I had not. I was in love with Keats, of course, and Shelley, and Leslie Howard, but none of these had ever weakened my knees. Life, I could see, held a lot in store for me yet.

Gina was a clever girl, very good on the arts side. We both wrote poetry and stories, and we read each other's efforts. But she had an advantage over me in that she could write and talk of love, which to me was still very much an ingredient of 'Idylls of the King'. We were both avid readers, but I was still immersed in the nineteenth century whilst she had moved out into modern fiction.

It was Gina who lent me a copy of Vera Brittain's 'Testament of Youth', and we discussed it at length. I day-dreamed of being a student at Oxford, just idly, not purposefully. In those days, as we knew from the book, merely to pass examinations was not enough. One needed a father with plenty of nous and a deep pocket. From Vera Brittain it was but a step to the reading of Winifred Holtby, and an extension of horizons in another direction. I owe a lot to Gina. She helped me to grow up.

To some extent the difference in our reading content may have been due to the fact that she belonged to the Boots' Library, whilst I was still using the free Library only.

Even more important to me was her slight knowledge, compared to my total ignorance, of modern poetry. We were getting no modern literature at all in school. Everything came to an end about 1900. Gina's boy-friend had lent her a book of modern verse and she read to me from Auden's 'Look Stranger'. I borrowed the book, and was excited by it, so for Christmas that year I chose 'A Little Book of

Modern Verse', and gradually became more familiar with the twentieth century idiom.

It was during this year in the Upper V that an event took place which seemed of shattering importance to us. Miss Luker had reached retirement age and would be leaving the school in July. We had never even given the possibility a thought. She and the school seemed an entity. I could not imagine one existing without the other. There were of course presentations, gatherings, well-deserved speeches of praise for her achievements. And there was the question on everybody's lips, "Who will succeed her?"

We liked the new head as soon as we saw her. She was young, attractive, modern in outlook, an arts graduate from Oxford. We saw things beginning to change, and we liked what we saw. Small prints of recent paintings and etchings appeared on the walls, to make way for which certain pictures of Greek and Roman busts, and of medieval frescoes were relegated to cupboards. The deputy head had still one year to go before her retirement, and she protested bitterly to her sixth form girls that these abominations were not art. It was a heart-breaking year for her, witnessing the thin end of the wedge being inserted, knowing that when she left the mallet would be applied with vigour.

But we appreciated it. We were pleased when the neat, conservative bindings of the reference library were brightened by new neighbours, some books of recent verse and a novel or two. We also enjoyed the half-an-hour a week spent in discussing current affairs with the headmistress, but the greatest change which we noticed was in the relationship between the new head and her sixth form girls. We felt suddenly grown-up.

CHAPTER TWENTY-SIX

Soon after Christmas that year our Guide Captain told us that a County Drama contest was being held, and that she would like our company to enter. The set scenes were from Shakespeare, and she had chosen the one from the 'Merchant of Venice'.

We were trained by a friend of Captain's, and we learnt our parts assiduously. As Lorenzo, I was entitled to wear the mauve satin tunic with red knickerbockers and red stockings. We had to take them home and come to the dress rehearsal wearing them, so I was able to model mine for the benefit of the family.

On the rehearsal day I had a severe cold. I had been to school as usual, knowing that if I stayed at home I would not have been allowed to go Lorenzoing in the evening. At break-time I stood in the Upper V formroom, clasping the fat, old-fashioned radiator, and shivering violently.

"If I feel as bad as this tomorrow I shall stay at home!"

"Hmm." Ruth said, with a slight sneer, "I wish I was allowed to stay at home every time I got a cold!"

A silly remark, as I always attended school throughout all my colds, but this time I was feeling really ill. Doreen and Norma were already lying, hot and damp together in their double bed.

I went to rehearsal, wearing my doublet and hose and shivering still. This was our very last chance to get everything perfect. I so wanted to do well, and I was doing so badly! We went over my part time and time again until the lady who was training us said,

"I don't know what's come over you tonight, Jane. You just aren't concentrating."

"I'm sorry. I don't feel well."

I was bundled into Captain's car, doublet, hose and all, and whipped off home. Nothing else mattered, the play, the competition, school, all moved into the hazy distance.

So now there were three of us ill in the bedroom. We did not talk, or eat. Each of us was a separate, suffering unit. In the intervals between the dreadful dreams of that night I was slightly aware of a strange sensation of the skin. By morning I was covered in a rash to end all rashes. We had scarlet fever.

Daddy came in before going to work and told us that the doctor would be coming to see us sometime during the morning.

"And don't be too upset if he wants to send you all away for a little while."

The doctor came, and gave his verdict, but decided that as we all had it, (by now Patrick was ill too), we could stay at home, but we were not to get up for a fortnight.

Poor Miss Laycock ran up and down the stairs faithfully carrying trays of food we did not want. The physical strain on her must have been heavy, although of course we were all bed-captives and out of mischief. Apart from the hard work I think she was happy whilst we were ill, because she felt indispensable, and we were quiet and grateful.

After about a week we were all feeling better, and wanted things to do. Miss Laycock brought us our dolls and we played together at mothers and babies.

My doll was called Anne, Norma's was Pearl and Doreen's was Kathy. Kathy had a painted face, and the eyes were depicted in a saucy, side-long look, so she soon developed a saucy, mischievous character. Anne was a good girl, and posh, because I was fifteen and knew how to make her so. Norma's Pearl was a loving, affectionate, disingenuous child. We made them talk in distinct voices, and all their narrated doings were in character.

The thing developed, of course. We each had a box for a doll's bed, and Miss Laycock brought us sewing materials and bits of rag, from which we fitted out the box beds with sheets, pillows, pillow-cases, knitted blankets and coverlets. Our babies were always properly put to bed in the evenings before we went to sleep ourselves.

There were some quiet times, when we were tired, or lazy, and at such times I would get out my latest book, 'Twenty Poems by Rudyard Kipling'. These I read and re-read, until I knew them almost by heart. The thin volume, covered in brown paper, is still in our bookcase, annotated in pencil with incredibly simplistic comments.

Eventually of course our days in bed were over and we were allowed to get up. The effect of this was to transfer all our doll-play downstairs to the living-room, where there was a table, more space, and many more tools available. Patrick was also with us, recovered, and delighted to have our company once again.

I received a letter from our Guide Captain, saying how sorry she was that I had not been able to be Lorenzo in the competition, but that our company had taken second place, and, she added,

"Please do not return the costume. I have had a word with the hirers, and they were not keen to have it back, as you did have scarlet fever actually in it. So I have settled with them and you may keep it."

Well, if it is now my own I might as well use it. We'll do a play. I'll be the prince, Patrick can be the page boy, and Norma can be the Princess. Doreen would rather be a fairy.

We were allowed no contact at all with anyone else, so we were entirely dependent on each other for company, and we spent hours arranging and producing a play, built around the four characters we had, and my doublet and hose. Miss Laycock was our only audience this time.

When the weather was fine we were able to go out in the garden for fresh air, but we had been used to freedom and soon began to feel confined in the small space. We asked Miss Laycock if we could go out on the green.

"Yes," she thought we might, "whiles the children is all in school. But you better come inside when they comes home."

So we went whooping and rollicking out to freedom, with our balls and skipping ropes and all our pent-up energy. After a few games along the conventional lines suggested by these toys we drifted along towards the bars, where we somer-saulted happily as we were wont. Gradually I became aware of a vast purple cloud on the horizon, which was billowing in our direction, not fast, on account of its immense size, but purposefully. Now it blotted out the sunlight altogether, and a voice from out the cloud said,

"Aren't you the lot who've had scarlet fever?"

It was the voice of Nitty Nora. Yes, I told her, we were the lot.

"So what are you all doing out here, smothering these bars with your germs? Other children are going to pick them up, and get ill. How long have you had it?"

We'd had it a month, I, as spokesman, told her.

"Well, then, you've got two weeks of quarantine left. Get indoors, all of you."

We trooped in, submissively, with me wondering how it was that, because we had been ill, we should also have to be humiliated. Thereafter we played in our own garden, or indoors, until we were out of quarantine. Fortunately our illness had begun at the start of the term, so Lucy was in no way involved.

A few days later I was again conscious of the call of the theatre and put on my Lorenzo outfit and wore it all the afternoon. By the evening I was once more covered in a brilliant rash, and thought I must have caught scarlet fever back from the costume. I did not however feel very ill, although there was a slight temperature and a headache. True to form, all the others developed bright rashes of their own, but none of us was really ill. According to the doctor this was german measles, although how four totally isolated children could have picked up an outside germ remains a mystery to me. That was the end of school for the rest of the term. The holidays came; all the children were at home all day, and we were free to mix with whom we would.

After the holiday I started back for the summer term, not giving a thought to any repercussions from my lengthy absence. Immediately I entered the formroom the deputy head, now my form mistress, asked me to take all my property and go down to the entrance hall and wait for her there on the bench. Slinging my not yet unpacked satchel over my shoulder I made my way, in some bewilderment, down the stairs and sat for a long time alone until assembly was over. My form mistress then came and asked me if I was now quite well. I assured her that I was.

"Before you put a single thing in our school desks, I want you to go home and spread them all out in the hot sunshine to get rid of the germs. We can not take any risks. You would not wish anyone else to have your long holiday, would you? Put your satchel out as well, and your shoebag. I suppose they've all been hanging around the house whilst you and your family have had every disease under the sun."

Again I felt humiliated. Apparently it was something rather common to catch scarlet fever, just as it was to belong to a large family, or not to be rich. I staggered home again with my load of books, and was given a not very effusive welcome on my re-appearance.

CHAPTER TWENTY-SEVEN

My last year at school was the year of the Silver Jubilee of King George V and Queen Mary, a year darkly overshadowed by events in Europe. As I walked down to the shops on Saturday, Tufnail's, the newsagents, were displaying the latest sheets on outside stands,

'Bombs on Abbyssinia.'

We were not so hardened to such headlines, and I felt sick.

It was for me, as for most, an anxious and stirring time, conducive to the writing of pages of verse, all of course in regular rhyme and metre. Although I was by this time reading modern poetry I was not then attempting to write it. It was a time of intensity. Gina and I found everything to be superlative, larger than life, greater than ourselves. We swung between elation and despair, and were always too immersed in either one or the other to see a funny side to it.

During one of these desparate times we wandered onto the school field and down among the shrubs, where we sat on the heavy garden roller, sucking grasses and sighing.

"I so want to go to college," Gina breathed, "and I know I shan't get the chance."

"I want to teach, and I can't possibly go to college either."

We plucked grasses moodily, enjoying our misery.

"Do you know, Jane," Gina said, "we're awfully alike really. We both know what we want, and we're both thwarted. We're both good at English, and we both have a second interest, only mine is art and yours is music."

"Yes, that's true, and we both love natural things, and being out of doors."

"I've written a new poem about my woods. I call them my woods, because no-one else ever goes in them. I'll let you read it, but not until you've seen my woods."

Gina lived at a farmhouse near Stockcross, and I often went out there on my very old sit-up-and-beg bicycle. That same evening, leaving the machine propped against the farmhouse wall I followed Gina across the muddy fields of spring and into the wood.

I saw what Gina meant. Tiny chips of green leaf were lined up on twigs, exposed roots of oaks had drawn over themselves a cover of fresh moss, pale green washed with silver. Everywhere I turned were inescapable primroses and violets growing overtly and confidently with nothing to fear. The air was cool with dampness and growth, and our own slow footsteps were the only sound to be heard, a light spasmodic snapping of twigs. We crept along in silence for a while, dipping under boughs undistorted by constant human visitation.

"If we sit here, I'll read you my poem."

We sat on the moss, both of us still in our navy tunics and white blouses, and Gina read me a delightful poem, whose inspiration was evident on every side. We talked, and we talked, each of us finding a temporary relief from the intensity of feeling caused by the impact of the future as it rushed towards us. We decided what was wrong with everything, with parents, with families, with schools, with governments, and rose from the moss like giants refreshed for battle.

"I do feel full." Gina told me.

"Why? Have you had too much tea?"

"Dinner! Mummy thinks I starve at school, so she always cooks me an enormous meal at night. Then when I've eaten it I sit down straight away to do my prep, and I can feel it all running to fat."

"Isn't it funny, people always think that plump people cannot possibly be either artistic or spiritual? There's still a tradition that a really talented person must necessarily look like a medieval ascetic."

Some of our friends were thin as grass blades, but Gina and I were cast more in the Rubens mould.

"I know, and yet surely a fat person has often had more, and not less, experience of life."

When we spoke of life we mentally spelt it with a capital 'L'. It was a key word, opening the doors to discussion of absolutely everything.

"But you have got a spiritual-looking face, Gina, pale and heart-shaped. Mine is just square."

"Well, never mind, Jane, you have got nice thick hair. Look at my mousy stuff! Men are very interested in hair. Have you noticed?"

I had not. Gina was years ahead of me in social development.

She walked with me and the tall bicycle as far as the road and we parted reluctantly. It was still only half-past-seven, but both of us had satchels bursting with homework.

A few days later I arrived home at the dinner hour to find Miss Laycock and my father having high words in the scullery. He was white with anger, and she was fiery red. My father had pointed out that something was dirty, and she had retorted,

"Do it yourself then. I'm not being told how to do things."

He told her that that was her job, her only job, and she shouted back that she was not paid enough, never had been paid enough, which was probably true. My father was angrier than I had ever seen him. He told her to go, any time, in fact the sooner the better.

"Get out of my house. I never want to see you in here again!"

She flounced upstairs to pack her few things. I was really frightened by now, and yet hoping it might be true. Fortunately the emotional strain was brief for all of us. My father had to get back to work, and we children to school, so what Miss Laycock did in the next hour or so I will never know.

I hurried home from school with a sense of foreboding. The house was empty, the dishes unwashed. So, putting on the kettle to remedy this, I began my new life as housekeeper.

The younger children came in, and we all had tea, sitting solemnly around the table and eating the scones Miss Laycock had made the day before. Although there was a heavy workload to be borne from this time on, there was also a sense of peace in the house. A weight had been lifted.

The morning after this strange day I told Gina as soon as I saw her what had happened.

"What!" she exclaimed. "No more ogre?"

"No more ogre. But a lot more work!"

"So it's just the family again? I'll bet you're glad!"

I told her, yes.

"Do you really think, Jane, that the family is the best social unit?"

"I don't know. What other social units are there?"

"Well, you've heard of the Russian experiments where babies have been taken from their parents at birth and brought up in super nurseries. They seem to do well enough."

"But they've been given no choice. Even when they have grown up they have had no experience on which to base a choice."

We drifted into the formroom, leaving the discussion to be taken up again later, or superseded by another.

In December of that year, 1935, King George V died. We still had no radio at home, so we read of it in the morning paper. It was the end of an era for many people. For me it was also the end of childhood. George V was the only monarch I had known, a kindly, grandfatherly figure, not so very unlike Devonshire Grandpa. His death was unbelievable, and I wrote a long poem on the subject. The Prince of Wales was now the King, and we transferred our loyalty and our love to this young and popular figure, who so soon ran into difficulties over his love affairs. Most people felt a deep sympathy for him and for his wife elect.

I was in Meg's house when he made his speech of abdication, just a year after the death of his father. Meg's mother was ironing, and she had left the wireless on to follow the news, which was completely given over to the King's problem, with a news reader standing by for the expected announcement. Three fine new pairs of winceyette pyjamas hung on the airing horse, newly made and pressed, for Meg was off to a London teaching hospital to continue her training as a nurse. She had left school the previous year, and had done some pre-probationary nursing.

"Three new pairs, Meg? What luxury!"

"Well, you know Mummy. She always says that two of anything is not economic."

"It's true, Jane." her mother said. "You need one in use, one in the wash and one in the drawer. Then they'll all wear longer."

I had great faith in Meg's mum's dictums. She was a wonderful housekeeper, strong on cleanliness and thrift, and a very kind, gentle person.

Meg had washed her hair, her brush and comb, and was packing a few things in a leisurely way. I knew she was longing for tomorrow, and to the real start to her career.

A voice spoke on the wireless, introducing His Majesty King Edward VIII. Meg's mum put down the iron. Meg stopped packing. I fiddled with the hinge of the writing desk and listened whilst history was being made. Although we had known what must happen we were shocked and saddened, as if by a personal tragedy. I wrote another poem that night.

114

CHAPTER TWENTY-EIGHT

Lucy had passed her London Matriculation, and had left Christ's Hospital. She wanted to be a nurse. Norma was fourteen, and was working behind the counter of a local chemist, enjoying her life and pleasing her employer. Doreen was settling in at the High School, and already meeting some of the problems which had bedevilled my own early days.

It was a time of very hard work. The Higher School examinations were drawing near, with four subjects to be taken. There was little time at home for studying, as Doreen and Patrick were still young, and not able to help except with minor jobs. There were meals to get, catering and shopping to do, washing which involved filling the copper and lighting the fire, ironing, and always more cleaning than could be fitted into the time. The evenings were taken up with one essential chore after another, until about nine o'clock, when the children had gone to bed. My father and I then had our cocoa quietly together and he would go up to bed.

"Well, goodnight my dear. Don't stay up too late."

"No, all right. Goodnight."

At last it was possible to start my prep, at ten fifteen. I used to work till midnight, go to bed, get up at six and finish it. Then I would get the breakfast, iron shirts and blouses needed for the day, pack my father's cheese sandwiches and get us all off to school. Norma could not do much to help, being only fourteen, and having such long hours.

I always liked getting to school, where it was warm, clean and tidy without any effort of mine. It seemed the easier part of the day. All the same, home was a happier place than it had been in recent years. Despite the hard work and the muddle, a peacefulness had returned to the family, and my father was decidedly more cheeful.

I enjoyed the school work too. We studied things in greater depth, and developed some critical sense. Most of our homework took the form of essays on account of the nature of the subjects studied, English, History, French. Biology required less writing, but no less work.

Towards the middle of the term our English mistress suddenly announced, "I want to find out how you are progressing in the writing of English prose, quite apart from your knowledge of chosen books. Write me an essay on . . . birds."

This was wonderful. It was freedom. I sat at home and wrote my essay on 'Birds', discussing their use as symbols, and their value to human beings, and handed it in the next day with a sense of a job well done.

When our books were returned and I opened mine I found that I had been given no mark at all. At the bottom of my essay a message was written in red ink

"You might at least have acknowledged your debt to this writer by some quotation marks at the beginning and end of this essay!"

At first I could not understand it. Then, as meaning seeped through, I reacted with a feeling of utter hopelessness.

After the lesson I approached her nervously with my essay.

"I didn't use any books at all. There's no need to look up anything to write about birds."

Silence.

"Oh, . . . well, you must admit it sounds rather like a book."

Silence again.

"However, that's not a very bad fault. Most books are fairly correct. Perhaps your work was a little formal, which gave me that impression."

She covered by giving me a little tutorial on the evils of imitating styles, and then dismissed me. The memory of that episode has made me very wary, as a teacher, of writing sarcastic remarks on children's exercise books.

It was my penultimate term at school. Christmas was over, and the dull time was upon us again. But the dullness this time was broken by a proposal of such brilliance that I cannot think of it even now without excitement. We were going on a school trip to Paris!

The project was broached by our French mistress in one of her lessons early in the term.

"We are taking a party to Paris in April," she told us, "so you'd better get out your rough books and pencils and take down all the details."

The pencils jiggled eagerly. I also wrote down the details, out of politeness and because there was nothing else to do, but without enthusiasm, as I had no intention of asking my father if I could go. We would be accommodated in a 'good second-class hotel', and would be taken around in a coach, with a guide to supply information. Three teachers were to accompany us, and we would be travelling via Folkestone and Boulogne. The details went on and on, my page filled up, and I could see with regret that we were not going to get on with any of the French romantic poets that lesson. We were doing Lamartine. When the bell rang it was time for break, and the wagging tongues wagged of nothing else.

As we came in from break and were changing our shoes in the cloakroom the French mistress said,

"I want to speak to you Jane. In my room at the end of the morning."

I could not think of anything I had done to warrant a reprimand. My prep was handed in, and was usually satisfactory. I had broken no rule as far as I could remember.

At half-past-twelve I knocked on her door and went in. She was never one to beat about the bush. We did not even sit down.

"I suppose there's no chance of your going to Paris, is there?"

Blunt, but I had to answer her.

"No. None at all."

"That's what I thought. Well, as it happens there will be one spare ticket, and we thought you might like to have it."

I cannot remember what I said. I felt like crying, and I think she knew, so she walked out, saying,

"Ask your father and let me know."

He would not be home until the evening, so I had to contain my excitement all through afternoon school. I walked home seemingly treading upon air.

Of course I was allowed to go, so I got out my rough book and studied all the details, those previously boring details which now seemed written in gold.

Our suitcases were not to exceed twenty inches in length, according to the literature we received. I scouted around among my friends and relatives and managed to borrow one of exactly that length. When we all met on the station most of the suitcases were considerably longer than mine, but it did not seem to matter.

School uniform was worn, of course, but each of us had brought a navy-blue dress to wear in the evenings. The journey seemed incredibly long. We started from Newbury station before nine o'clock, and did not arrive in Paris until about nine in the evening, by which time I was so tired that nothing seemed real.

Breakfast was the first revelation. We were served the usual croissants and butter, with a choice of coffee or chocolate. The coffee was so strong that many of the girls wished they had done as I had done, and chosen chocolate.

Each day there was a coach trip to one or several of the well-known sights of Paris, Notre Dame, Monmartre, Versailles. All the things we should see were assiduously covered, and the postcards piled up on our dressing-tables. The guide who accompanied us everywhere was a young man, tall, good-looking, which together with being French made him very interesting to a group of English eighteen-year-olds. We all pestered him for his autograph, and to sign our postcards.

We had been told before leaving England that we would be expected to speak in French at all times. A few girls made tentative attempts to practise now and then, but when we were all in the coach the chattering sounded like an English garden party. I was luckier. I had chosen the seat next to the driver, a middle-aged, family type of man, and he could understand and answer my school French. He was not an educated man like our girls, but it was interesting to hear him talk of his home, and his children, and he liked me to tell him of my family.

In the evenings we changed into our navy dresses for the main meal of the day. I was intrigued when one evening oranges were served for dessert, because they still had stems and leaves attached.

One of the girls was making her bed in the morning when she found a grub under the pillow. She screamed and yelled until one of us came and removed it.

"Hadn't we better look under the mattress?" I asked, "to see where it came from?"

Between two of us we turned the stiff, horse-hair mattress right over, and there, in the middle, was a large family of grubs using a hole in the ticking for a front door.

"I can't sleep on that! I refuse to sleep on that!"shrieked the girl, who had already spent two deeply restful nights upon it.

We did not blame her. One of us told the mistress, who saw the manageress, who came and looked at it, grubs and all, without emotion, took it up in her arms and carried it away. She sent a maid with another.

In most of the historic buildings we visited there was original furniture all clearly labelled and roped off from the public. I made a point of sitting, if only for a second, in all the chairs of famous people, just by lifting the tasselled rope. Thus I came home proudly and truthfully claiming to have sat in Victor Hugo's chair, Napoleon's chair, Marie Antoinette's and several others.

One evening was spent at the 'Comedie Francaise', where we saw 'La Boheme'. I enjoyed it in a way, but would have preferred to see a straight play. I found the opera form unconvincing, especially when the consumptive heroine, a large hefty singer, lay dead upon the stage panting hard and visibly.

The evenings, after the excitements of the day, were dull, true guest-house lounge type of evenings. We had been told to bring a book to read, so, dinner over, twenty or so navy-clad girls thronged into the drawing-room each clasping a good book chosen to impress, but not much reading was done. There was plenty to discuss, and we were always happy to talk, talk, talk.

We arrived back at the hotel at about six o'clock one evening, after a busy day in Fontainbleau, and went to our shared rooms to change. There was a little packet on my bed, addressed to me. It was very light, with a Newbury postmark, and when I opened it out fell a shower of wilting wild violets, white and purple, such as I had often picked along the Enborne Road with my sisters. Norma had enclosed a little note -

"In case you are homesick, a few violets we found on Sunday."

I was not homesick, but I was touched. Of all the girls around me, with their easy, normal homes, not one of them had received violets from an English lane in April.

The holiday ended, as all holidays must, and we took our experiences and our postcards home. It had been unforgettably romantic and thrilling. I have never been to Paris since then.

Back at school of course, at the beginning of my last term we inevitably had to write a French essay about our trip. I was delighted with this assignment, and wrote freely. Apparently I wrote correctly as well, because it was marked with a first. At the bottom was a little note in red ink -

'Ah, ce que c'est que d'aller à Paris!'

The term sped; examination time drew near. I worked as hard as circumstances allowed. The evening before we began I said to my father,

"Our exams start tomorrow."

"What exam is that then, dear?"

"The Higher School Certificate, you know, like the other one, only harder."

"Well, good luck. It's nice to get an education."

So we sat, and we worried, and when they were all over we left school, results as yet unknown. I had reached Upper VI, was the school secretary, and had become acceptable, neat, conforming, but the price had been paid. I was also diffident, gauche, and quite without self-confidence.

I am deeply grateful to both my schools for the education they gave me. Of course there was not the variety and breadth of syllabus which today's schools must offer, especially as in those days boys and girls were almost always segregated, but for thoroughness and depth the teaching I received was second to none.

Gina and I went round the building on that last day taking leave of the teachers we loved. We were in tears as we said 'Goodbye', although the Staff seemed to stand up bravely to the parting.

Each girl went in separately to take leave of the headmistress.

"Well, goodbye, Jane. It's been nice to have known you."

"Goodbye, and thank you very much for all your help."

"Not at all. What do you hope to do now?"

"Well, I really want to be a teacher, uncertificated, of course."

"Oh. Well, I hope you get what you want. Let us know how you get on."

We shook hands, and I left.

On the day after leaving school I tramped around Newbury trying to get a job in a shop. No-one wanted me.

Life is change. Only death is static. It is not only the educational scene that has changed. Newbury is different in its social structure, its outlook, its amenities and its population. Its appearance has changed so greatly since I was first aware of things that although many of its oldest and dearest features remain the same, large areas of the town and its surroundings require a strenuous effort of the mind to reconstruct in the mind's eye what once was there. Even the Parish Church clock has turned blue in the face.

THE END

118